# NO JUST CAUSE

## The Law of Affinity in England and Wales: Some Suggestions for Change

*A Report by a Group Appointed by the Archbishop of Canterbury*

CIO PUBLISHING
Church House, Dean's Yard, London SW1P 3NZ

**ISBN 0 7151 3697 6**

Published for the Archbishop of Canterbury and the General Synod of the Church of England by CIO Publishing

Typesetting by Dorchester Typesetting Group Limited
Printed and bound by The Friary Press Limited, Dorchester & London

# Foreword by
# The Archbishop of Canterbury

In recent years there have been suggestions, from a number of quarters, that the law which prevents marriages between those connected through affinity, i.e. by marriage but not by blood, should be changed. The matter received prominence in the years 1979-82 when on four occasions Private Members' Bills were introduced in the House of Lords to amend the present law. It seemed to me that, before the question was further debated, it would be helpful if a thorough study of this matter could be made in which the theological, sociological and legal aspects could be carefully examined and the experience of other countries taken into account.

I am grateful to Lady Seear and her team for the work which they have done. This is a difficult subject, which touches deep instincts in people, and it is not surprising that the Group have come up with both a majority and a minority report. I hope that both will be carefully studied, not only within the Churches, but by all who are concerned with the essential role which the family must play in the fabric of our society.

+Robert Cantuar

*Lambeth Palace*
*London*                                    *6th April 1984*

i

# Contents

# Members of The Group

The Baroness Seear, BA, HON LL D, HON D.Litt,
Visiting Professor in The City University

The Rt Hon. Sir George Gillespie Baker, OBE,
Formerly Judge and President of the Probate Divorce and
Admiralty Division (from 1971 the Family Division) of the
High Court of Justice

The Rev. G. R. Dunstan, MA, HON DD, FSA,
Professor Emeritus of Moral and Social Theology in the
University of London; Honorary Research Fellow in the
University of Exeter; Canon Theologian Emeritus of Leicester
Cathedral

Ruth Finnegan, MA, D.PHIL, Diploma in Anthropology,
Reader in Comparative Social Institutions, The Open University

R. J. C. Hart, MB, F.R.C.PATH,
Consultant Medical Microbiologist, Member of the House of
Laity of the General Synod

Ruth Hook, MA,
Parent and author

Janet Mattinson, BA,
Member of Society of Analytical Psychology, Chairman of the
Staff Executive, Institute of Marital Studies, Tavistock Insti-
tute of Medical Psychology

The Rev. O. M. T. O'Donovan, MA, D.PHIL,
Regius Professor of Moral and Pastoral Theology in the
University of Oxford and Canon of Christ Church

iv

Joan Rubinstein,
In private practice as a solicitor and analytical psychotherapist


*Secretaries to the Group*
The Rev. M. H. Atkinson, MA,
Research Officer, Board for Social Responsibility of the General Synod

L. P. M. Lennox, LL B,
Solicitor, Assistant Legal Adviser to the General Synod

# Preface and Terms of Reference

Your Grace,

In May 1982 you invited us to consider the law of affinity in England and Wales under the following terms of reference:

(a) To review the working of the present law bearing on the marriage of persons related by affinity, taking account of theological, sociological and legal issues and of the practice in other States

(b) To consider whether any general modifications in the law are called for in modern circumstances and/or

(c) Whether exceptions should be allowed in particular cases and, if so, according to what criteria and by what procedure these should be authorized.

We held our first meeting in June 1982 and met on twelve occasions. We invited evidence generally from the public and more specifically from particular authorities which we identified, or which were recommended to us. On two occasions we heard evidence orally. A list of persons and organisations who submitted statements to us or whom we consulted appears in Appendix VII. We wish to thank them all.

We found our task an interesting but difficult one, and our Recommendations touching the existing law are not unanimous. A Minority Report from three of us is in Chapter 13.

We have the privilege and pleasure of submitting this our Report.

| | | |
|---|---|---|
| Seear | Ruth Finnegan | Janet Mattinson |
| George Baker | Robert Hart | Oliver O'Donovan |
| Gordon Dunstan | Ruth Hook | Joan Rubinstein |
| January 1984 | | |

# CHAPTER ONE
## Introduction

1. The Archbishop's initiative in setting up a group with these terms of reference was taken as a result of a number of Bills introduced in Parliament in recent times.

2. Under present law, a man and woman who are related as step-parent and step-child are prevented from marrying one another because they are within the prohibited degrees of affinity as set out in the *Marriage Act 1949*. Between 1979 and 1982 four Bills attempted general reform of the law in this area. The first three Bills were introduced by the Baroness Wootton of Abinger. Each sought to remove the remaining prohibitions on marriage between persons related by affinity (i.e. by marriage). These Bills would have had wider consequences than a subsequent Bill introduced by the Lord Lloyd of Kilgerran which was limited in its application to step-parents and step-children only. It sought to enable a court to give leave to a step-parent to marry his or her step-child. None of the four Bills has succeeded in becoming law.[1]

3. There have been other items of legislation in Parliament in this area of law during these years. Since 1979 three separate Personal Bills have been promoted, each of them successfully, by three different couples to enable them respectively to marry. The effect of each Bill,[1] once enacted, has been to provide that the subsequent marriage of the particular couple is lawful and valid. Such marriages would otherwise have been unlawful and void because in each instance the two persons concerned were

---

[1]For further information about each Bill see Appendix II.

1

related by marriage and within the degrees of affinity which constitute in law an impediment to marriage.

4. All these Bills – both the Private Members' and the Personal ones – aroused considerable interest both inside and outside Parliament. And yet there has not for many years been any thorough study of the marriage law as it affects people related by affinity.[2]

5. During the course of the House of Lords Second Reading debate on the *Marriage (Step-parents and Step-children) Bill* introduced by Lord Lloyd, the Archbishop's initiative was announced on 22nd February 1982 by the Lord Bishop of Hereford (The Rt Rev. John Eastaugh) in these words:

> If the view prevails that this Bill does not provide a way forward that is workable, the Archbishop of Canterbury has authorised me to say that he intends to set up a committee to advise him on this matter in consultation with the other Churches. What seems to be needed is a thorough, careful study of the matter in which theological, sociological and legal interests would be represented and in which the experience of other countries could be taken into account, with the aim of seeing whether some alternative to the present Personal Bill procedure can be devised . . . but I mention the intention of the Archbishop of Canterbury to set up this committee since it shows that the Church recognises that there is a problem which needs some solution, and that solution needs to be found. What we are looking for is a means by which, without sweeping away the present law, cases can be looked at and adjudicated against some reasonable criteria. If the present Bill is judged not to provide a workable answer, the setting up of such a committee might be a helpful next step.
>
> (*Hansard* House of Lords, 22nd February 1982, at column 790)

---

[2]It seems the last study of this topic in this country was by another group appointed by a previous Archbishop of Canterbury, the Most Rev. Cosmo Gordon Lang, whose report entitled *Kindred and Affinity as Impediments to Marriage* was published by SPCK in 1940. The terms of reference of that Commission included consanguinity or kindred relationships as well as those of affinity. It was intended to inform the thinking of the Anglican communion as a whole, and to be available for the information of a Lambeth Conference in 1940. The Second World War caused the conference to be postponed to 1948, and by then interest in these questions seems to have receded, since the record of the proceedings, including ten pages of Committee report on *The Church's Discipline in Marriage*, makes no reference to the 1940 study.

In consequence of the Archbishop's action, Lord Lloyd withdrew his Bill. This Report is the work of the Group set up by the Archbishop following the Bishop of Hereford's announcement.

## Our Use of Terms

6.   For the purpose of this report the terms 'consanguinity' and 'affinity' are understood as follows. Relatives by consanguinity or kindred are persons to whom one is related by blood either of the whole blood or half blood or by legal adoption. Relatives by affinity are the spouse or former spouse of any of one's relatives and any relative of one's spouse or former spouse; and in this report the term 'affine' is used to denote persons related by affinity. 'Affine' thus includes both in-laws and step-relations. These are definitions of the general use of the words consanguinity and affinity. Legislative provisions relating to consanguinity and affinity define them more precisely (see paras 10-34). The Terms of Reference of the Group exclude consideration of consanguinity.

7.   The Group's consideration of the issues and main arguments involved the use of the term 'family'. Differing understandings of this term have caused confusion in the past. In this Report we use two terms to refer to the family: the 'primary family' and the 'extended family' which are fully described in paragraphs 83-84.

8.   A 'child of the family' is a child under the age of eighteen, not being a child who has been boarded out by a local authority or voluntary organisation (i.e. a foster child), who has at any time lived in the household of another person and been treated by that person as a child of his or her family.

9.   'Intervening spouse' we define as the party to a marriage, which has been already terminated by death or divorce, through whom two persons are related to one another by affinity.

3

# CHAPTER TWO
## The Law Today

10.   The law of marriage in different parts of the United Kingdom does not have the same origin, and the present civil law of marriage in England, Wales, Scotland and Northern Ireland is not enacted in the same statutes.[3] The *Marriage Acts 1949-83* comprise the law of marriage in England and Wales. The principal Act is the *Marriage Act 1949* which does not generally extend to Scotland and Northern Ireland (section 80(2)). The law of marriage in Scotland is quite distinct in its origin and development from the law of marriage in England, Wales and Northern Ireland and is now comprised in the *Marriage (Scotland) Act 1977*. Since 1978 the substantive law in Northern Ireland has been the same as in England.

11.   It is important and desirable, that, where possible, the law of marriage should be the same in all countries of the United Kingdom. Another Gretna Green or reverse Gretna Green complication should be avoided. We have been anxious, therefore, that our conclusions and recommendations should take note of the existing law in Scotland and Northern Ireland as well as that in England and Wales.

12.   It is also necessary to examine the canon law of the Church of England touching marriage: it is part of the law of the realm and binds the clergy of the Church of England. The regulations of the Church of England being domestic to that

---

[3]For the Channel Islands and the Isle of Man see Appendix V.

4

Church are not the same as those of other Churches and religious bodies in the United Kingdom.

13.   It should be noted that the Archbishops of Canterbury and York have no jurisdiction over any other Church in the United Kingdom. The Church in Wales, the Church of Ireland and the Scottish Episcopal Church constitute independent provinces in the Anglican Communion and are not part of either the Province of Canterbury or the Province of York. The established Church of Scotland is, of course, Presbyterian in government.

## A.   England and Wales

14.   The *Marriage Act 1949* section 1 as amended provides

> 1. – (1) A marriage solemnized between a man and any of the persons mentioned in the first column of Part I of the First Schedule to this Act, or between a woman and any of the persons mentioned in the second column of the said Part I, shall be void.

15.   The First Schedule to the Act as amended by the *Children Act 1975* section 108(1), Schedule 3, para 8 is as follows:

KINDRED AND AFFINITY

PART I

Prohibited degrees of relationship

| A man may not marry his: | A woman may not marry her: |
| --- | --- |
| mother | father |
| adoptive mother or former adoptive mother | adoptive father or former adoptive father |
| daughter | son |
| adoptive daughter or former adoptive daughter | adoptive son or former adoptive son |
| father's mother | father's father |
| mother's mother | mother's father |
| son's daughter | son's son |
| daughter's daughter | daughter's son |
| sister | brother |
| wife's mother | husband's father |

5

| | |
|---|---|
| wife's daughter | husband's son |
| father's wife | mother's husband |
| son's wife | daughter's husband |
| father's father's wife | mother's mother's husband |
| mother's father's wife | father's mother's husband |
| wife's father's mother | husband's father's father |
| wife's mother's mother | husband's mother's father |
| wife's son's daughter | husband's son's son |
| wife's daughter's daughter | husband's daughter's son |
| | son's daughter's husband |
| son's son's wife | daughter's daughter's husband |
| daughter's son's wife | |
| father's sister | father's brother |
| mother's sister | mother's brother |
| brother's daughter | brother's son |
| sister's daughter | sister's son |

16.   It must be noted that Part I of the Schedule includes both consanguineous and affinal relationships. The first 9 and the last 4 relationships in each column are consanguineous and therefore beyond the terms of this report. Prior to the *Marriage Act 1949* nineteenth century case law[4] had established that the *Table of Kindred and Affinity* (Archbishop Parker's Table see para 21) annexed to the Book of Common Prayer, which was imposed by the *Act of Uniformity 1662*, was the authoritative expression of the prohibited degrees. The *Children Act 1975* added the relationships of adoptive or former adoptive mother, daughter, father and son to the columns. An adoptive brother may marry his adoptive sister.

17.   No person may marry within the degrees expressed in the above list, and all marriages purported to be made within these degrees are void. On giving notice of intention to marry, any declaration which is false renders a person liable to prosecution under the *Perjury Act 1911*.

18.   There were significant changes in the general law relating to affinity during the first 60 years of this century. The *Deceased Wife's Sister Marriage Act 1907* allowed a man to marry his

---

[4]See footnote on page 48.

deceased wife's sister. A woman was enabled to marry her deceased husband's brother by the *Deceased Brother's Widow's Marriage Act 1921*. (The widow's deceased husband's brother is a parallel relationship to the future husband's deceased brother's widow.) Then the *Marriage (Prohibited Degrees of Relationship) Act 1931* allowed marriage with the spouse of a deceased niece, nephew, aunt or uncle. All these reforms, therefore, affected persons related by affinity though only where the spouse or relative had died. The law relating to marriage was consolidated by the *Marriage Act 1949* which when first enacted provided in section 1 as follows:

1. – (1) A marriage solemnized between a man and any of the persons mentioned in the first column of Part I of the First Schedule to this Act, or between a woman and any of the persons mentioned in the second column of the said Part I, shall be void.

(2) A marriage solemnized between a man and any of the persons mentioned in the first column of Part II of the said First Schedule, or between a woman and any of the persons mentioned in the second column of the said Part II, shall not be void or voidable by reason only of affinity.

(3) A marriage which by virtue of the last foregoing subsection is not void or voidable if solemnized after the decease of any person shall be void if solemnized during the lifetime of that person.

Part I of the Schedule is reproduced in paragraph 15. Part II of the Schedule was as follows:

PART II

*Statutory exceptions from prohibited degrees of relationship.*

| | |
|---|---|
| Deceased wife's sister | Deceased sister's husband |
| Deceased brother's wife | Deceased husband's brother |
| Deceased wife's brother's daughter | Father's deceased sister's husband |
| Deceased wife's sister's daughter | Mother's deceased sister's husband |
| Father's deceased brother's wife | Deceased husband's brother's son |
| Mother's deceased brother's wife | Deceased husband's sister's son |
| Deceased wife's father's sister | Brother's deceased daughter's husband |

| Deceased wife's mother's sister | Sister's deceased daughter's husband |
| Brother's deceased son's wife | Deceased husband's father's brother |
| Sister's deceased son's wife | Deceased husband's mother's brother |

19.   The most recent change in the law was made by the *Marriage (Enabling) Act 1960* which extended to persons related by affinity through a spouse or a relative whose marriage has been dissolved by divorce the reforms made by the three Acts passed earlier in this century. This act repealed sections 1(2) and (3) and Part II of the First Schedule of the 1949 Act and provided in its own Section 1 as follows:

> 1.  Certain marriages not to be void
>
> (i) No marriage hereafter contracted (whether in or out of Great Britain) between a man and a woman who is the sister, aunt or niece of a former wife of his (whether living or not), or was formerly the wife of his brother, uncle or nephew (whether living or not), shall by reason of that relationship be void or voidable under any enactment or rule of law applying in Great Britain as a marriage between persons within the prohibited degrees of affinity.

20.   Thus since 1960 persons who were within Part II of the First Schedule to the *Marriage Act 1949* may lawfully marry whether the intervening spouse is alive and divorced or dead.

CANON LAW

21.   A table of kindred and affinity for the reformed Church of England was first set forth by authority in 1563. In the *Code of Canons of 1604* marriages which breached the impediments were declared to be 'incestuous and unlawful and consequently shall be dissolved as void from the beginning'. The table was based on the relationships referred to in Leviticus 18 and became known as *Archbishop Parker's Table*. It was printed with the Book of Common Prayer until amended by the Convocations when the revised form was substituted. The modern canon of the Church of England promulged in 1969 is in the following form:

*Canon B 31 Of Certain Impediments to Marriage*

1.  No person who is under sixteen years of age shall marry, and all marriages purported to be made between persons either of whom is under sixteen years of age are void.

2.  No person shall marry within the degrees expressed in the following Table, and all marriages purported to be made within the said degrees are void.

## A TABLE OF KINDRED AND AFFINITY

| A man may not marry his: | A woman may not marry her: |
| --- | --- |
| mother | father |
| daughter | son |
| adopted daughter | adopted son |
| father's mother | father's father |
| mother's mother | mother's father |
| son's daughter | son's son |
| daughter's daughter | daughter's son |
| sister | brother |
| wife's mother | husband's father |
| wife's daughter | husband's son |
| father's wife | mother's husband |
| son's wife | daughter's husband |
| father's father's wife | father's mother's husband |
| mother's father's wife | mother's mother's husband |
| wife's father's mother | husband's father's father |
| wife's mother's mother | husband's mother's father |
| wife's daughter's daughter | husband's son's son |
| wife's son's daughter | husband's daughter's son |
| son's son's wife | son's daughter's husband |
| daughter's son's wife | daughter's daughter's husband |
| | |
| father's sister | father's brother |
| mother's sister | mother's brother |
| brother's daughter | brother's son |
| sister's daughter | sister's son |

In this Table the term 'brother' includes a brother of the half-blood, and the term 'sister' includes a sister of the half-blood.

(This list is not identical with that in the Book of Common Prayer of 1662 in that it adds the adopted son or adopted daughter. Note that the first eight and last four relatives in both lists are kindred i.e. consanguineous, and not affinal, relations.)

22.　Persons to be married may give notice to the incumbent of the parish of the Church of England or the Church in Wales in which they reside (or in which they have their names on the electoral roll) that they wish banns to be published and, if certain basic requirements are complied with, the clergyman is obliged to publish them (*Marriage Act 1949* section 8). Section 12 of the *Marriage Act 1949* provides:

> . . . . where banns of matrimony have been published, the marriage shall be solemnized in the church . . . in which the banns have been published.

23.　For the clergyman of the Church of England or of the Church in Wales, the only exception from the strict *obligation* to marry any parishioner who requests his ministrations is in the case of a subsequent marriage of a divorced person who has a former partner still living and here the general law gives him a *discretion* whether or not to officiate. Maintaining a provision introduced by statute in 1938, the *Matrimonial Causes Act 1965* section 8 provides:

> No clergyman of the Church of England or the Church in Wales shall be compelled:
> (a) to solemnise the marriage of any person whose former marriage has been dissolved and whose former spouse is still living; or
> (b) to permit the marriage of such a person to be solemnised in the church or chapel of which he is the minister.[5]

24.　If in the future statute and canon law were to diverge the Anglican clergyman might find himself obliged to marry two

---

[5]Regulations made by the Convocation of Canterbury (October 1957) and by the Convocation of York (June 1938) advise a clergyman of the Church of England not to solemnise the marriage of a divorced person who has a former partner still living. These Regulations do not form part of canon law but the clergy are expected to pay due regard to these solemn Acts of Convocation. Breach of the Regulations does not constitute an offence under the *Ecclesiastical Jurisdiction Measure 1963*.

people who come within the prohibited degrees according to canon law but who nevertheless are enabled by statute to marry. In such circumstances the obligation upon the clergyman could be relieved by the statute providing him with a discretion. Alternatively if the canon law were to be amended to conform with the statute there would be no conflict of obligations facing the Anglican clergyman.

25. The non-established Churches are not under the same obligation to marry those who present themselves and therefore, if it were contrary to the discipline of his or her Church, a minister could refuse to marry persons who were related within the present prohibited degrees.

## B. Scotland

26. The *Marriage (Scotland) Act 1977* comprises the law of marriage in Scotland. For the purposes of this enquiry it is necessary to consider the relationship between the civil law of marriage in Scotland and the criminal law of incest in that country.

27. The present crime of incest in Scotland is defined in the *Incest Act 1567*, (which explicitly incorporates the 18th chapter of Leviticus as extended by the courts) and the *Criminal Procedure (Scotland) Act 1938*. Incest is committed by a male or female person who has intercourse with persons related as follows:

| *Relatives of male person* | *Relatives of female person* |
|---|---|
| (a) by consanguinity | (a) by consanguinity |
| Mother | Father |
| Daughter | Son |
| Grandmother | Grandfather |
| Granddaughter | Grandson |
| Great grandmother | Great grandfather |
| Great granddaughter | Great grandson |
| Sister | Brother |

| Aunt | Uncle |
| Niece | Nephew |
| | |
| (b) by affinity | (b) by affinity |
| | |
| Mother-in-law | Father-in-law |
| Daughter-in-law | Son-in-law |
| Grandmother-in-law | Grandfather-in-law |
| Granddaughter-in-law | Grandson-in-law |
| Step-mother | Step-father |
| Step-daughter | Step-son |
| Step-grandmother | Step-grandfather |
| Step-granddaughter | Step-grandson |

28.    These lists include the same relatives by affinity for each sex as are contained in the First Schedule to the *Marriage Act 1949* set out in paragraph 15 of this Report although the modern terms of in-laws and step-relations are used. The restrictions upon consanguineous relationships apply whether these are of the half blood or full blood and thus extend to cover half-brothers or half-sisters of a parent, and children of a half-brother or sister. With regard to relationships by affinity it appears that, for the purposes of incest, the relationship remains within the forbidden degrees even after the marriage which created the relationship has ceased to exist. Under the present law, a degree of relationship which is not prohibited for the purposes of marriage cannot act as a prohibited degree for incest (*Criminal Procedure (Scotland) Act 1938* section 13). The *Children Act 1975* provides for Scotland that 'on the making of an adoption order the adopter and the child shall be deemed to be within the said prohibited degrees in respect of the law relating to marriage' (Schedule 2 paragraph 1(3)). This provision touching adoption is parallel to that in the *Children Act 1975* in the law of England (para 16).

29.    Unlike the law in England and Wales, the Scottish law of incest is not restricted to sexual intercourse between relatives by consanguinity only. Certain relatives by affinity are also included. Thus an examination of the Scottish law of affinity requires an examination of the criminal law of incest in Scotland, bearing in mind the desirability of maintaining

harmony between the civil law of marriage in England and
Scotland. A ridiculous position would result if the forbidden
degrees for incest were wider than the forbidden degrees for
marriage. Any reform of the law of affinity in England and
Wales ought to take note of the law of incest in Scotland so that
the situation may be avoided in which two affines who contract
a lawful marriage south of the border would be guilty of incest
if at any time they chose to live in Scotland. In England sexual
intercourse between affinal relations is not a crime.

30.   We were greatly assisted by and much interested in
the *Scottish Law Commission report No. 69* entitled *The Law of
Incest in Scotland* (Cmnd. 8422) which was published in
September 1981. The Commission's principal recommendations included:

> 6.   The crime of incest should not be constituted by intercourse
> between a person and the relatives of his or her spouse.
>
> 7.   It should be a separate offence for any step-parent or former
> step-parent to have sexual intercourse with his or her step-child under
> the age of 16 years.
>
> 8.   If any person over the age of 16 years is in a position of trust or
> authority in relation to a child under 16 years and is a member of the
> same household, it should be a criminal offence for that person to have
> sexual intercourse with the child.
>
> 11.   The maximum penalties for incest and for the offences contained in
> Recommendations 7 and 8 should be as follows (a) on indictment in the
> High Court – life imprisonment; (b) on indictment in the Sheriff
> Court, (unless remitted to the High Court for sentence) – 2 years
> imprisonment; (c) on summary conviction in the Sheriff Court – 3
> months imprisonment.

(These recommended penalties for the offences contained in
Recommendations 7 and 8 are higher than those provided for
cases concerning children of the same ages where there is no
consanguine or affinal relationship or position of trust or
authority).

31.   It is important to note that the Commission was

concerned with the law of incest in Scotland only,[6] and not at all with the law of marriage. However, some of the recommendations if implemented would affect persons related by affinity and were therefore of interest to us.

32.   The combined effect of these recommendations would be to remove from criminal sanction in Scotland sexual intercourse between a male or female and those of his or her relatives listed in (b) in paragraph 27 except in so far as it takes place between a step-parent or former step-parent and his or her step-child under the age of 16 years. Thus, if the step-child is 16 or over, intercourse will no longer be incest. However, the Commission recommends a new criminal offence where any person over the age of 16 in a position of trust or authority in relation to a child under the age of 16 who is a member of the same household has intercourse with that child.

## C. Northern Ireland

33.   The origin of the law of marriage in Northern Ireland is similar to that in England. Following disestablishment of the Church of Ireland in 1869, the *Matrimonial Causes and Marriage (Ireland) Amendment Act 1870* transferred the matrimonial jurisdiction exercised by the former ecclesiastical courts of Ireland to the civil courts.

---

[6]In England and Wales it is an indictable offence for a man to have sexual intercourse with a woman whom he knows to be his granddaughter, daughter, sister or mother. It is immaterial that the sexual intercourse took place with the consent of the woman. It is an indictable offence for a woman of the age of sixteen or over to permit a man whom she knows to be her grandfather, father, brother or son to have sexual intercourse with her by her consent. On a person's conviction of incest against a girl under the age of eighteen or against a boy under that age, or of attempting to commit such an offence, the court may by order divest that person of all authority over the girl or boy. If that person is the guardian of the girl or boy, the court may remove him or her from the guardianship, and may appoint a person to be guardian of the girl or boy during his or her minority or any less period. (*Sexual Offences Act 1956* sections 10, 11 and 38 as amended by *Guardianship Act 1973* section 1 (8).)

34.   Article 61 of the *Matrimonial Causes (Northern Ireland) Order 1978* made similar reforms to the *Marriage (Enabling) Act 1960;* it declares that a marriage between a man and certain of his divorced wife's relations or the divorced wife of certain of his own relations shall not be void. Other departures from Archbishop Parker's Table[7] which correspond to the English legislation of 1907 and 1931 had been enacted for Northern Ireland by the *Marriage (Prohibited Degrees of Relationship) Acts (Northern Ireland) 1907-1949.*

---

[7]The *Act of Uniformity 1662* which imposed use of the Book of Common Prayer was repealed in relation to Northern Ireland by the *Statute Law Revision Act 1950.* However, its repeal did not affect the law relating to affinity in Northern Ireland. Archbishop Parker's Table had been incorporated in the corpus of law by nineteenth century case law: see footnote on page 48.

# CHAPTER THREE
## The Personal Bill Procedure

35. Standing Orders for the House of Lords provide that a Personal Bill may relate to 'the estate, property, status or style, or otherwise . . . to the personal affairs of an individual' (*Erskine May* (19th edn) pages 1014 and 882).

36. The main clause in the Personal Bills introduced by the three couples used the following formula:

> Notwithstanding anything contained in any enactment or any rule of law to the contrary, there shall be no impediment to a marriage between . . . and . . . by reason of their relationship of (stepfather) and (stepdaughter), and no marriage hereafter contracted beween them shall be void by reason of that relationship.

37. The history of the jurisdiction of Parliament in these matters was rehearsed by the Lord Chancellor, Lord Hailsham, in a speech during the second reading of the *Edward Berry and Doris Eilleen Ward (Marriage Enabling) Act 1980*. Until the Reformation the Church had granted dispensation in individual cases. In the sixteenth century this power was removed from the Papal Courts and assumed by the Crown in Parliament. Thus the Personal Bill was a perfectly proper instrument to use (*Hansard*, House of Lords 22nd May 1980, at column 1059). The procedure was more widely used in the past, principally for making certain family property rearrangements, naturalising aliens, and, nearer our field, for divorce, until a simpler procedure became available in 1857. From late Stuart times until the *Matrimonial Causes Act 1857* (which first transferred jurisdiction in relation to divorce from ecclesiastical courts to the Queen's courts) the total number of Private Acts passed to

16

dissolve marriages is put at 317.[8] From 1857 until the passing of the *Matrimonial Causes (Northern Ireland) Act 1939*, many Private Acts were passed to dissolve marriages of persons domiciled in Ireland. The effect of each of these Personal Acts was to alter the marital status of the persons to which they related.

38.　In 1947 a petition was presented to the House of Lords on behalf of a Mr Stevenson for leave to bring in a Bill to enable him to marry the former wife of his brother whom she had divorced but who was still living (such a marriage was then forbidden on grounds of affinity, becoming permitted only under the *Marriage (Enabling) Act 1960*). The Personal Bills Committee which considered the application reported that the circumstances of that case were not sufficiently strong to justify exemption from the general law and the Bill did not proceed.

39.　In this century the Personal Bill procedure had been little used before 1979. Solicitors in private practice are not trained to promote Bills in Parliament and do not commonly do so. The same solicitor acted for each of the three couples who brought Personal Bills in 1980 and 1982: he is aware of the procedure because he is one of the few who practise in parliamentary agency.

40.　Procedure by Personal Bill in Parliament is the only means at present available to enable two persons related by affinity to be dispensed from the existing prohibited degrees and enabled to contract a lawful and valid marriage. There is neither judicial process nor administrative procedure available to them.

41.　We consider that the Personal Bill procedure gives rise to serious difficulties. First, as we have said, it is little known. Until these three Personal Bills were presented it is likely that couples who sought legal advice on the matter were told that there was no remedy available to them and that they could not contract a lawful marriage in any circumstances.

---

[8]*Putting Asunder: A Divorce Law for Contemporary Society* (SPCK 1966), page 84.

42.    Second, the procedure involves considerable costs for the couple. In 1983 the costs were likely to be in the region of £2500 to £3500. Assistance under the *Legal Aid Acts 1974 to 1979* is not available for this procedure.

43.    Third, the three Personal Bills attracted much publicity which presumably each of the three couples would have preferred to avoid.

44.    Fourth, the procedure by Personal Bill affords no opportunity for statements to be tested or challenged. Without in any way suggesting that the statements submitted by any of the three couples in support of their respective Personal Bills were inaccurate or incomplete there is room for criticism of a procedure which does not provide for the kind of testing and examination of the parties and their evidence which a court would provide. In each of the three actual instances of successful Bills, the intervening spouse had died. The Group was concerned that if the intervening spouse had been divorced but still living there could have been an opportunity for collusion between the couple, or for duress upon the intervening spouse, which the procedure by Personal Bill might not have exposed.

45.    Fifth, one may reasonably ask how opponents of a Personal Bill would set about opposing it. They would have to lobby Members of Parliament or Peers to seek to have the Bill amended. Furthermore the couple who are the subject of the Bill would have no opportunity of speaking to defend allegations or criticisms, unless by chance they happened themselves to be members of one or other House.

46.    Sixth, the three Personal Bills seemed to be an inappropriate use of Parliamentary time, in that the general goodwill and support for them and the ease of passage which they enjoyed suggest that they might satisfactorily have been resolved by a less exalted and preoccupied tribunal.

47.    The Group generally agreed that the procedure by Personal Bill in Parliament is an unsuitable mechanism to decide whether two people should be allowed to marry one another.

# CHAPTER FOUR
## Issues Facing the Group

48.   The Group met for the first time in June 1982 and issued a public invitation for written representations. Individual invitations were sent to recognised authorities, to specialist groups and societies and to representatives of the major Christian and non-Christian religious bodies with members in Britain. As a result statements were received from a wide range of sources and Appendix VII lists all the individuals, groups, societies and religious bodies which submitted written statements.

49.   We now set out without comment some of the arguments which we received in favour of retaining or changing the existing law. Representation received in favour of abolishing completely the present prohibitions on marriage between persons related only by affinity (as the Bills introduced by Lady Wootton would have done) was not extensive, but it came from authoritative quarters and was of some strength.

### Arguments by Religious Bodies

50.   Arguments for retaining the status quo came from several religious bodies. Their reasoning relied on a variety of theological, social and psychological considerations. They argued that the marriage tradition is divinely sanctioned and therefore should not be changed. The divine sanction should determine the law of the land and should apply to all persons without exception. Other religious groups and bodies drew a distinction between the law of the land and their own internal disciplines. They would continue to expect adherents to conform to the rules laid down by their faiths, without regard

to freedoms to marry which might be permitted by the law of the land. This view was advanced on behalf of Christians of the Orthodox tradition, of Jews and Muslims.

51. Our attention was drawn to Biblical texts. In the New Testament, 1 Corinthians 5 was quoted to us, with St Paul's clear denunciation of the church for not expelling a member who had taken his father's wife. Some Christian groups grounded their position on the Mosaic law as they read it in the Old Testament of the Bible (Lev. 18 and 20 and Deut. 27). They considered that the effect of those texts is to declare that marriage creates a new psycho-social unity – one flesh – which includes not the couple only but also in-laws and other step-relations. Those new relationships are not dissoluble by death or divorce. Jews in this country also take as the basis for their marriage those same texts. Other groups were aware of the Mosaic texts but did not regard them as unambiguous in their meaning, or as being incontestably binding upon modern practice. Others again believed that their intention and rationale were social rather than religious.

52. Statements received about Islam and from Sikh and Hindu groups seemed to ground their practices sometimes upon social argument and sometimes on a more exclusively religious base, though the two were not always distinguishable. Where the base was religious, moreover, the regulations enforced in the countries of origin of these beliefs varied greatly from those of English law.

## Social and Psychological Reasons

53. Most of the arguments against any change could be described as either social or psychological. Some of them came from religious groups, but were not strictly religious in nature. They may conveniently be arranged according to the party to whom it was expected harm would come.

### INDIVIDUAL HARM

54. It was argued that full human maturity requires that people should be free to develop adult relationships outside the

family. The strength of family relationships, either of affection or of revulsion, may interfere with the freedom of members to mature into true adulthood and personal independence. The tradition of marrying outside the household is broadly observed across most human cultures. It is strongly buttressed by law and is conducive to personal adult independence and responsibility. To permit marriage or to open up the prospect of marriage within the present prohibited degrees may lead to relationships within which the parties fail to grow and develop fully as persons.

HARM TO OTHER MEMBERS OF THE FAMILY

55. Many representations expressed concern about the effect that an alteration in the law would have within the family. (These statements did not always lead in the direction of maintaining the existing impediments; sometimes they argued for modification, while continuing to oppose total abolition.)

56. In our society, it was represented, children are nurtured from a state of complete dependence to that of a desired independence in adulthood and the most important nurturing institution is the family or household. On this view, the sex relationship is held to be one in which mature and independent persons are able to give themselves fully to each other. Except between the spouses such a relationship is not attainable within families or households, where members need from each other a kind of love and affection, protection and education, which in most human societies is held to preclude sexual relationships. This inhibition is sometimes called, loosely, the incest taboo, though our correspondents were not always aware of the variations on the boundaries that that taboo can be shown to have in different societies, and to have had historically in our own. Where the parties are not related by blood, as in the case of in-laws and step-relations, similar inhibitions are said to apply, manifesting themselves in feelings of repugnance or disapproval of sexual relationships. It is these feelings, the social needs of households and the emotional needs of their members, which underlie many of the specific issues to which

our attention has been drawn. Witnesses feared the effect any alteration of the law would have upon:

> step-children under the age of eighteen in a household, if they become the object of sexual advances by a step-parent which that step-parent intends, or expects, or hopes, one day to lead to marriage (sexual intercourse with children below the age of sixteen is of course a criminal offence);

> the children, infant or adult, or other persons within a household, where one of their number is singled out for this kind of affection, or where one rather than another initiates it;

> the roles established by an earlier marriage where there is a subsequent marriage e.g. can a father continue to perform the role of father when by marrying his step-daughter he becomes in addition brother-in-law both to his natural children and any other step-children? In such a case do the children lose their father in any important sense? Another example might be the effect upon children (and adult relations) if a mother divorces her husband and marries his father – he who was once, say, simply a grandfather becomes in addition a step-father.

57. There were strongly expressed views that our family tradition was vital for society as a whole, both economically and psychologically, but that many factors were undermining it. An alteration in the laws relating to the impediments on marriage between affines would be one more such assault on the family and its effect would perhaps be to destroy what was left and to increase breakdown, precipitating any one of a number of possible personal and social aberrations.


HARM TO SOCIETY GENERALLY

58. It was argued that the law has been for a long period in steady retreat from regulating social relationships, that this area is being progressively abandoned to unbridled individualism,

and that the removal of these impediments would be a further development in what is an undesirable direction. Further diminution in social regulation of the marriage relationship is undesirable both in itself, and because of the encouragement it would give to those seeking further relaxation of the social restraints upon selfishness and individualism. For the Group to stand firm at this point and support the present law on the marriage of affines would be to help to stop the juggernaut of individualism in its tracks.

59. It was argued that the institution of the family needs firm boundaries for its support, and that such boundaries include the present clear and traditional marriage regulations. To alter the definition of the marriage relationship would, it was said, undermine much more widely the foundations of the family.

60. It was suggested that incest is regarded in our society with a revulsion which is firmly expressed in criminal law. Relationships within the bounds of affinity while not incestuous in a biological or legal sense do, it was said, arouse in the public's mind something of the same sense of revulsion or outrage. Marriages within those boundaries would be a public scandal to which the law ought not to lend support.

61. It was also argued that one of the functions of law is to clarify relationships through definition. An alteration in legal status alters the social significance of what is altered, and also the meaning of related persons or institutions. If the impediment to marriage with in-laws were to be removed, the whole notion of in-laws would become changed. People would no longer relate to the parents of their spouses or the spouses of their children as they now do, to the impoverishment of the whole notion of family.

## Alignment with the Criminal Law

62. In England and Wales and Northern Ireland (though not in Scotland: paragraphs 26-32) sexual intercourse between step-parents and step-children and between other affines is not

forbidden by the law (unless the children are under 16); nor where two (unrelated) people have been cohabiting is it forbidden for one of them to marry the child of the other person. It is thus argued that it is anomalous that while sexual intercourse is not illegal when practised between two persons who are not married either to each other or to anyone else, those persons may not marry. This argument was used by Lady Wootton during debate on the *John Francis Dare and Gillian Loder Dare (Marriage Enabling) Act 1982*.

### Inequities in the Present Procedure

63. The three Personal Bills presented to the House of Lords showed that if sufficient determination and money are available dispensation from the present law can in appropriate circumstances be obtained. Legal aid is not available for this process. It is inequitable, it was maintained, for dispensation to depend on such accidents. This liberty ought to be available to all, and the simplest way to achieve that is by abolition of the impediments.

### Unsuitability of Possible Alternative Procedures

64. Possible alternatives to the Personal Bill procedure would be administrative decision by a superintendent registrar, or a judicial decision in an appropriate court. However, law generally permits people to make their own decisions about marriage, and it was therefore argued that it would be invidious in these few cases for the exercise of what is otherwise a general liberty to depend either upon the non-reviewable decision of an administrator or upon some kind of investigative process in a court. People wishing to marry ought not to have to argue for their liberty.

### Lessons from History

65. Whatever the origin of the impediments on affinity, it is clear, said some statements, that in medieval times they became

extended and elaborated by canon lawyers in order to provide grounds for annulment of marriages when the law on what is now called divorce had not been developed. Until 1835 marriages within prohibited degrees were prima facie valid, but voidable. Since 1835 such marriages have been void. As we have seen, subsequent legal changes have taken outside the impediment of affinity some relationships which in 1835 were retained within it. There is clearly legislative freedom in this field, and there is no reason, it was argued, why further changes should not be made to enable affines of marriageable age to marry. It is already clear that the increased incidence both of divorce and remarriage is also increasing the probability of step-relations wishing to marry one another.

## Marriages Contracted in Ignorance of the Impediments

66. It was argued that with the increasing numbers of step-relationships present in society comes an increased chance that people will marry others who fall within the prohibited degrees, in ignorance of the legal impediment which exists. Lady Wootton reported one case where the impediment was discovered only after banns had been called in church and wedding guests invited. Marriages contracted in ignorance are in law void, and the legal status both of the parties themselves and of any children they may have is reduced. The discrimination which the law makes against such 'marriages' contracted in ignorance is, it is argued, inequitable, and could be removed if such 'marriages' could become, in fact, true marriages recognised by the law through the removal of the disqualifying impediments.

## Freedom to Marry

67. Just as one argument in favour of retaining the present impediments is based on the alleged undesirability of promoting further individualism in marriage, so here, conversely, it

25

was said that in many fields of law over the last century and a half there is a trend for statutes to enlarge individual freedoms and the same trend ought to be followed here too. There is no case, it was said, for restricting it at this point any more than in the other relationships which have been legalised since 1907. Moreover, in an increasingly plural society it is difficult to justify grounding social policy upon the Old Testament which many religious groups would not accept as part of their tradition, or when, if they do, they would differ in regard to the meaning or application of its rules.

## The Experience of Other States and Cultures

68.  It was submitted that some other states with systems of law derived in large part from the common law of England have no impediments against marriage between affines, with no obvious damage to their family structure or the fabric of their societies. For example, Australia abolished these impediments in 1975 and about half of the states in the United States of America appear never to have had such impediments. The experience and practice of other states is elaborated in Chapter 7.

69.  In addition, it emerged from the anthropological evidence that while there are always rules and prohibitions relating to marriage and sexual relations, these vary greatly according to the general patterns of kinship and of social organisation in each culture (see Appendix VI). Rules or taboos about marriage and sex between affines are particularly varied. It may be argued that there is no universal validity for the affinity rules in this country, which are represented in the existing legal impediments, and that there are different ways of ordering relationships between affines without any consequent breakdown in family life.

# CHAPTER FIVE
## The Tenor of the Group's Discussions

70. The Group recognised that the success of the three Personal Bills in Parliament in 1980 and 1982, with the support of Bishops, gave rise to a variety of problems. It demonstrated that power to dispense from the general provisions of statute in particular cases existed, and that goodwill may sometimes be found for such dispensation. However, that procedure is subject to a number of serious criticisms which we have described in paragraphs 41 to 46.

71. Our discussions came to centre on a small number of issues. First, it was accepted that there were certain types of case where marriage between persons at present prohibited from marrying might be permitted. For instance, the parties may be of mature years (as were the three couples who presented Personal Bills) and all other interested parties may also be of mature years and readily giving assent. The parties may at no stage have effectively lived together within a single household in circumstances such as to raise any suspicion that the proposed marriage might be undertaken with anything less than free and full consent. In cases like these the Group had little difficulty in adopting a preliminary position that procedures ought to be provided cheaply and readily for such persons to marry. Given agreement on this point, the major question for consideration was whether the general impediment should be retained, with or without some procedure for dispensation according to some guidelines which would need to be elaborated, or whether there should be a change in the general law in some direction to be recommended.

72. There was also general agreement on cases where there were step-children in a household. It was recognised that sexual feelings and fantasies (sometimes fully conscious, sometimes less so) exist within families, as do strong rivalries, jealousies and hatreds. Hatred and revenge can be expressed through the initiation of sexual relationships with either the hated person's partner or child. The Group was reluctant to expose children to an atmosphere in which they might regard themselves or be regarded as a potential marriage partner. We accepted the possibility that if the impediments to marriage were to be removed, illicit sexual relations within the family might be more likely to occur than under present law. Many of the representations received warned of the dangers of such a development, and the Group's discussion of the case for and against changes in the law took serious account of this possibility.

73. On the other hand, most but not all of us had less difficulty in envisaging the law permitting marriages between a person and his or her parent-in-law, grandparent-in-law, son or daughter-in-law or grandchild-in-law should they wish to marry. It was less easy to object to marriage within such relationships *per se*. In the nature of these cases we have been unable to envisage situations in which the younger party, while under the age of 18, could have been a child of the family of the older party. Objections on that ground are, however, to be distinguished from other objections to marriage with in-laws. Some of us believe that a problem about ambiguities in relationships arises if in-laws marry. This problem is developed later in paragraphs 108-110.

74. A concern not only for personal liberty and responsibility but also for the maintenance of the family and of marriage as valued institutions in our society was common ground between us. Indeed, questions relating to the maintenance and well-being of family life based on marriage provided a constant focus for our deliberations. Different points of view, both within the Group and in representations made to us, concerned specific questions such as precisely where the

boundaries of 'the family' are or should be drawn, the rationale for these boundaries, how to assess certain changes or diversities and how particular statutory provisions would be likely to affect specific aspects of family life. The importance which we attach to the concept and practice of lawfully instituted family life is emphasised as we feel it right to make clear the assumptions on which the Group worked. We were conscious that the value of the family is challenged by some schools of thought, for example certain anarchist, Marxist or feminist groups who have advocated radical change in the current patterns of marriage and the family, even their abolition.

75.   There was one other general point which we bore in mind. As a body reporting to the Archbishop we were conscious of the reservations which clergy of the Church of England and the Church in Wales might feel about an obligation to marry affines, if that should be recommended. Our principal concern is of course with the general law but we felt the importance of considering the conscience of the clergy and suggest a provision for it later. The number of affines seeking to marry would surely be very much smaller than the number of divorcees, but a problem of conscience for clergy might very well remain.

# CHAPTER SIX

## The Group's General Consideration of the Main Arguments

### Arguments for Maintaining the Existing Impediments

ARGUMENTS SUBMITTED BY RELIGIOUS BODIES

76.   In considering the representations submitted by religious bodies, the Group recognised that it is concerned solely with the general or secular law of marriage and with recommendations for its change or reform. The United Kingdom is a plural society comprising different religious and cultural groups. It would be impossible, even if it were desirable, for secular law to attempt to reflect differing rules surrounding the many marriage customs and traditions reported to us. We have already noted the special legal position and responsibility of the Church of England as the established church of the land (paragraphs 22-24). So far as other Christian denominations and other religious groupings are concerned, we conclude that it must be for them to determine their own marriage disciplines with regard to affines if they disapprove of any changes in the general law.

77.   As a Group set up by the Archbishop of Canterbury we have been particularly concerned with the Biblical record. It has been suggested that St Paul's rebuke to the church in Corinth (1 Cor. 5) for not expelling a man who had taken 'his father's wife' is an unambiguous instruction for Christians today. One may presume that the text is referring to the man's stepmother and thus, it has been argued, this text constitutes a

definitive prohibition for Christians on marriage between step-relations, certainly in the ascending line.

78. New Testament scholars and commentators discuss variously the translation of the verse, the meaning of which turns on St Paul's use of the Greek verb *echein*. The English versions of verse 1 read:

> *Authorised Version*: 'It is reported commonly that there is fornication among you, and such fornication as is not so much as named among the Gentiles, that one should have his father's wife.'

> *Revised Version*: 'It is actually reported that there is fornication among you, and such fornication as is not even among the Gentiles, that one of you hath his father's wife.'

> *Revised Standard Version*: 'It is actually reported that there is immorality among you, and of a kind that is not found even among pagans; for a man is living with his father's wife.'

> *New English Bible*: 'I actually hear reports of sexual immorality among you, immorality such as even pagans do not tolerate: the union of a man with his father's wife.'

The word *echein* was as common as 'to have' is in English today. The difficulty facing interpreters and translators of the text is to know whether the couple with whom St Paul was concerned had married or were cohabiting.

79. Close examination of the different Bible versions of the verse shows that translators do not believe that the man had married the woman in question. None of them has translated the verb *echein* to mean 'to marry'. The New English Bible's phrase 'the union of a man with his father's wife' gives no indication of whether they were married or not.

80. To try and clarify the matter one must go to the Greek text. This leads us to the same conclusion as the Bible translators. The plain sense of the Greek text does not require marriage to be assumed. The use of *echein* nearest in usage to the one with which we are concerned seems to be in 1 Cor. 7.2

31

where *echein* is used in the context of sexual touching; it is better that a husband and wife should 'have' one another, in sexual embrace, for the avoidance of *porneia*. Most commentators accept that *porneia* is used widely of illicit relationships generally and not narrowly of fornication only. In our view the most realistic interpretation of 1 Cor. 5.1 is to accept the same association: the offender 'has' his father's wife i.e. his step-mother in sexual embrace. The force of the present infinitive in the Greek rather than the aorist tense means that the idea is 'living with' i.e. a continuing union and not a temporary one.

81.    Our conclusion, therefore, is that the most straightforward reading of the text is that the man and woman were 'living together' as the Revised Standard Version says i.e. in an illicit union rather than in lawful marriage. Had St Paul wished to write of their union as a marriage, he had – and used in other contexts – unambiguous words with which to do so. The relationship cannot be termed incestuous. On this supposition we do not find it necessary to read this verse as directly bearing upon the question whether or not marriage with step-relations should be legalised, and it is this question, different from the one which St Paul was addressing, which is the subject of our enquiry.


SOCIAL AND PSYCHOLOGICAL REASONS

82.    The representations supporting retention of the existing legal impediments which most impressed the Group argued that for social or psychological reasons individuals or family relationships may be harmed by reform of the general law of affinity particularly in respect of step-parents and step-children.

83.    One set of problems we had to face concerned the different senses in which the key term 'family' is often used. This is a complex and emotive area in which terminologies and interpretations are not fully agreed, and one of the characteristics of families in modern Britain is their variety. Nevertheless we found it useful to distinguish between two main senses in

which the term is used. For some the term 'family' refers to the primary family group sharing the same home, typically parents (or a single parent) living together with their dependent children in one household (the technical term being the 'nuclear family'). This is broadly the definition of 'family' in government statistics. For others the term 'family' includes also the wider network of relations (through both kinship and marriage) who normally do not reside in the same household but are nevertheless regarded in a varying measure as members of the same family.

84.   We found it helpful to emphasise the distinction between the two different concepts of family. Certain proposals might well be significant for the continued maintenance of healthy relationships and development within the 'primary family' group living together, but of relatively little relevance for 'extended family' groupings and relationships.

85.   Certain of the arguments presented by some psychologists, social workers and others – which, at least at first sight, seemed to tell strongly against any change in the present system of prohibitions – related to the effect on individuals within the 'family'. But it was noted that the sense of 'family' referred to in most if not all of these representations seemed to be the primary domestic group living together – the one in which a child is likely to grow up and mature. Insofar therefore as this danger might indeed be one to be guarded against, it is important to look at relationships within the primary family (which can include step-children) rather than to the wider extended family or network of relatives. The potential dangers of sexual liberty within the close family circle were also mentioned in some of the anthropological evidence which stressed, among other things, the common practice in most cultures of marrying outside the household. One possible explanation for this custom is the importance of avoiding disruptive erotic interests within the primary family and protecting young children from sexual exploitation by those in authority over them (see Appendix VI). We acknowledge the strength of this evidence.

86.   There is growing interest and concern about child sexual abuse in this country, meaning by this term the involvement of immature children in sexual activities which they do not truly comprehend and to which they are unable to give informed consent. Reliable figures about the extent of this abuse are not available. In line with other statistics about crime, it is likely to be much more common than most people, including the police, realise. A recent survey estimates that at least 1500 cases occur every year.[9] Awareness of the extent of child sexual abuse is probably about as limited now as was awareness of physical child abuse until the last decade or so.

87.   We agreed that sexual intercourse between members of the primary family other than between husband and wife could put at risk the freedom of both the two persons concerned and other members in the same family to mature into true adulthood and personal independence. These arguments influenced our final recommendations.

88.   We recognised that in this field as in many other areas of social policy, the relation between law and behaviour could not be assessed with any certainty. A change in the law might or might not affect sexual behaviour within the close family. It could be argued that any removal of the present prohibition on marriage between step-relations (and perhaps other affines) would prima facie encourage, or at least remove a curb on, such sexual interest. It could also be maintained that the existence of such rules does not necessarily prevent infringement of them. Law is not a matter carefully considered by a couple before engaging in sexual intercourse (except, perhaps, with regard to the age of consent) and is of no relevance to their sexual feelings or fantasies. The present prohibitions might even in some cases actually encourage sexual relations initiated by either partner, secure in the knowledge that such relations could never lead to marriage.

---

[9]See the 1981 report 'Child Sexual Abuse' published by the *British Association for the Study and Prevention of Child Abuse and Neglect.*

89.   Despite this uncertainty we attached great importance to the protection of the younger members of a family, i.e. children under the age of eighteen years, from exposure to sexual advances by older members of the same family. Various provisions of the criminal law specifically protect children below the age of 16 years but there are no particular criminal protections for young people between the ages of 16 and 18 years. We considered the question whether some young people aged between 16 and 18 would be at risk if the general law were changed to allow, for example, a stepfather and step-daughter to marry. A young person in this age group may make sexual advances towards or receive them from a step-parent considerably older than himself or herself and we asked whether the younger person whilst physically mature might be under powerful pressures to make decisions which might later be regretted. As is well-known, physical maturity may be reached a long time before psychological, emotional and social maturity, and we wished there to be some protection available for young people.

90.   We considered whether it was possible for the law to provide some protection for the younger person in these circumstances if the general impediment on marriage between affines was substantially reformed or abolished. Two alternative forms of protection might be possible: either the existing impediment in these circumstances would not be removed or reformed at all (and thus any marriage would be void) or the law could delay the lawful marriage for a specified period of time.

91.   If the law did seek so to protect the younger person in these circumstances we recognised that the necessity for such protection would have to be weighed against the infringement of the freedom or right to marry which inevitably would result from such constraints.

92.   We considered that the arguments set out under the heading 'Harm to Society Generally' (paras 58-61) are difficult to assess. While not supported by scientific evidence they

35

represent sincerely and strongly held views based on traditions not lightly to be discarded.

93.   This was a question that we considered very seriously indeed. It was clear from the public discussion of the topic, including the debates in the House of Lords on the various Bills introduced since 1979 (Appendix II), that any apparent threat to the basic values and structure of the institution of the family is perceived as a matter of the deepest concern not only to the more extreme traditionalists, but also to a wide range of deeply serious and open-minded commentators.

94.   The most helpful approach developed from distinguishing clearly between the issues arising in the primary or nuclear family as distinct from the extended family. In the primary family its members live together and see each other intensively on a daily basis, the household in which they live is 'home' (a rightly emotive word), and children grow up and develop as mature members of society in a context which is as far as possible free from sexual rivalries. We accept that the primary family is also often the locale of great unhappiness, bitterness and at times frustration, but at the same time it forms the context for mutual affection and support, and for the rich and healthy development of human beings. It is also the focus for great personal commitment from its members, who not infrequently invest a great deal of themselves in the personal relationships typically developed in the surrounding of the home, not least in the bringing up of children. The typical pattern in modern Britain – probably dating back for some centuries – is that such primary families live in separate independent households, set up at the time of the marriage.[10] The British pattern thus contrasts with that in certain other societies where a young couple do not set up a home separate

---

[10]There are exceptions, particularly in time of housing shortage or financial pressure, when a young couple must begin their married life in their parents' household. The extent of this is not known precisely, but it can be assumed to be the exception rather than the rule (one indication is that only 1% of households in Britain in 1981 consisted of 2 or more families – *Social Trends 1983* Table 2.2.) and is certainly not the desired pattern.

from the parental generation on marriage (this latter pattern is most typically found in a number of non-industrial societies, often accompanied by more widely applicable kinship terms, and marriage prohibitions among affines). In the British context it is within the primary family that relationships are at their most intense and, correspondingly, most vulnerable.

95.   We accept that the present system of rules and prohibitions regarding marriage is indeed relevant in the maintenance of the primary family and the system of blood relationships which upholds it. There was no suggestion of any changes in the prohibited degrees of consanguinity and to that extent therefore no threat to the integrity of the primary family.

96.   It should also be remembered that in the increasing number of cases of separated or divorced parents, children may sometimes move between two households, spending some time in the home of each of their natural parents. Joint custody orders are becoming more frequent. While the relationship of child and natural parent (consanguines) would, of course, be unaffected by any change in the general law relating to marriage between affines, the whole question of step-families, and in particular the relationship between step-children and step-parent, is treated more fully below in paragraphs 103-104.

97.   The wider extended family appears to function rather differently. This consists not just of close relatives such as one's parents, brothers and sisters, or grandchildren but more distant relatives such as cousins, great-uncles, nieces, second cousins, third cousins and so on, in principle *ad infinitum*, together with the spouses of all these relatives. In practice, members of this wider family grouping do not – in contrast to the primary family – live together in the same household, and seldom do the relationships assume the same intensity as for those interacting constantly on a daily basis. Furthermore some links are stressed more than others, and though this partly depends on the closeness of the kinship tie (blood relations such as parents, siblings or grandchildren, for example, tend to be

37

more consistently important) this is not the only factor: how far and when such links are activated may also depend on such other factors as geographical distance, job, interests, personality, or particular needs at a given time. The closeness of the relationship between two people, whether they are related by blood or marriage, is affected by these factors: while some links are often of great importance, the closeness or otherwise of particular relatives is affected as much by personal choice as by theoretical kinship ties. This somewhat individual approach to links in the extended family network in Britain contrasts with that of some other societies (particularly in non-industrial cultures). In some societies large extended families live and co-operate together as in a sense a joint unit and links set up by marriage between two such large family groups may be treated as a kind of permanent affinal alliance between the two families as separate entities. Thus sometimes members of two family groups are bound into a system of rules (including marriage prohibitions – and sometimes prescriptions – between certain members of these groups). The kinship system in modern Britain does not take this form (and perhaps never has), so that affinal ties relate primarily to individuals rather than whole families and may not in practice outlast the marriage which brought them into being.

98. Given this background, we had to ask ourselves how relevant were the existing impediments in maintaining the mutual support and related functions so valuably carried out by the extended family, and which we wished not to undermine.

99. On this central question, various arguments were advanced. On the one side it was argued that any change in the present prohibitions of marriage between particular affines would dilute the strength of these extended family ties and hence undermine their function; further that relationships in general among affines would be altered if the impediments to marriage between affines were to be removed to the impoverishment of the whole notion of family, and that this would be a high price to be paid for extending the personal freedom of particular individuals to marry. Conversely it was argued that,

given the way extended family ties worked, the question of whether two people related by blood or affinity could or could not contract a lawful marriage seemed to be of little relevance to their functioning in practice. There seemed to be little differentiation between the strength of relationships (and consequent mutual support and concern) as between say, cousins (who can marry), aunts and nephews (who cannot), fathers-in-law and daughters-in-law (who at present cannot), brothers-in-law and sisters-in-law (who once could not but who now can). The implication was that other factors were of equal or greater importance than whether or not marriage was legally allowed between the two parties.

100.   We concluded that the legal impediments play little part in the everyday relationships between members of the same extended family group. For example, a woman helping to care for the ageing grandfather of her husband is unlikely to have much room for concern about whether or not there is any legal impediment preventing her marrying the grandfather in the (somewhat unlikely) event that they should ever so desire, any more than an uncle entertaining his nieces and nephews is likely to be sparing much thought for the fact that the law does now allow him to marry their mother (his brother's wife). Such examples present little difficulty. More disturbing possibilities were mentioned in representations to us. What about a father who is becoming sexually interested in his son's wife? Or a young married man who begins to feel he might prefer not his own, perhaps immature, wife but her more mature mother? We recognised that such cases could arise and probably already do from time to time (though given that the parties are not normally living in the same household they may be rarer than is sometimes supposed); it was certainly not unreasonable to fear that such cases might be encouraged by any change in the law. Our general feeling was that the law cannot prevent such cases arising. There was no evidence to suggest that removal of a number of affinal impediments earlier this century had had such effects but similar fears had been expressed at the time. Nor is there any evidence that these statutory reforms have undermined the ties of mutual support and affection.

101. After very careful consideration and bearing in mind the possibility of extreme cases a majority of the Group agreed that the retention of the existing impediments on marriage between in-laws is not essential to the maintenance of healthy and stable relationships. Thus we do not accept the argument that abolishing these impediments would tend to 'undermine the family' (in the sense, here, of the extended family).

102. We think that marriage between in-laws would in practice be rare (although there is no statistical evidence available to support this view) and that most people might still prefer to avoid them (in much the same way that marriage between cousins has been lawful for centuries but many people still feel uneasy about it). Couples might choose to apply greater restrictions than those prescribed by law (particularly perhaps those guided by the disciplines of specific religious denominations), but this is not a reasonable argument for prohibiting the lawful marriage of such in-laws as do wish to marry.

103. A second important area of consideration was the category of step-families – those, that is, which contain two or more step-relations in the same family. Such families are not all of one kind. Some share certain characteristics of the extended families and some are more analogous to the co-residential primary family. Where, as sometimes happens, step-relations do not live together in the same household and have never done so (as for example with some of the individuals concerned in the Personal Bills), it seemed reasonable to a majority in the Group to adopt the same view as for the extended family relationships (para 101): i.e. to regard legal restrictions as irrelevant for the maintenance and conduct of such relationships between adults.

104. The situation is different in the case where the step-relations are or have been living together in one household. This happens frequently, for example a wife or husband living with the child or children of the spouse's former marriage in the role of step-parent to the step-child(ren). This situation is in some respects similar to the primary family group, particularly

as regards the need to avoid sexual interest within the family circle and to protect a child growing up in that family from sexual influence by those in authority over him or her. The situation is slightly different from the usual primary family in that a step-parent may not wholly replace the natural parent. Indeed as we have already noted in paragraph 96 current thinking seems to regard it as important for a child to retain contact with the natural parent whenever possible. So long as the step-child was growing up under the authority of a step-parent and being treated as a child of the family, the Group unanimously agreed that the existing impediments on marriage should be retained. In these circumstances the impediments do contribute to the protection of the child's long-term interests and the reduction of any risk to the integrity of the household.

105. A majority of us agreed that the impediment on marriage between step-parent and step-child should not be a permanent lifelong prohibition and felt that the fundamental freedom to marry should not be indefinitely denied to a couple so related. On the younger person's attaining years of maturity the two persons, as adults, should be free in law to marry. Such a provision was not seen as likely to lead to any general ill effects on the family.

106. Finally in our considerations of the family, we felt bound to take cognisance of the representations from the few couples related by affinity who wished to marry but were prevented by law from doing so. The prohibition on their being able to marry had caused all three couples who had promoted Personal Bills unhappiness, disappointment and frustration.

107. Although members of the Group could not agree about the nature and extent of protection which the law should provide for affines within the primary family, the Group did agree that the legal impediments should be retained so long as the younger person was a child of the family.

108. There were three other arguments relating to the possible harm to society generally which were submitted and

considered by us. The first argument concerned relationships between affines generally, and in particular the risk of role conflict or ambiguity and confusion in such relationships. Before considering this argument it is helpful to acknowledge that it is not clear how far and in what sense one's affinal relationship arises. For example, the general law in England provides that the in-law relationship is not terminated by divorce or death of one's spouse and so a husband's mother-in-law is still his mother-in-law after his marriage is dissolved or after his wife's death. Does the subjective 'in-law' relationship necessarily continue however throughout their joint lives or is it severed by the death or the divorce of the spouse? The duration of any true sense of relationship depends on the circumstances of the case: the depth and breadth during the marriage of the relationship between the spouse and the parent-in-law, the relationship of any children of the family with their grandparents and the circumstances of the termination of the marriage. On the termination of the marriage or on death contacts may continue unchanged, or fade slowly over a period of time, or be ended abruptly.

109.    It was suggested that relationships in general between affines would be altered if the impediments to marriage were to be removed resulting in either the impoverishment of the whole notion of the family or at least difficulty for some individuals. The difficulties which role conflicts might cause did not seem to us to be substantial enough to outweigh the arguments in general terms for people's liberty to marry, but seemed the kind of problem of coping with personal relationships which people are generally able to resolve in their own lives. The one possible exception was the position of a child in the family holding the simultaneous (or rapidly succeeding) roles of child and spouse to the elder step-relation; this exception strengthened our wish to retain a limited restriction on marriage in such cases.

110.    A possible further reason underlying the fears about the effect of possible role conflict following any further relaxation in the current restrictions seemed also to rest on a possibly not

fully explicit feeling that the generations should be kept apart in marriage and that this principle would be threatened, perhaps with consequent chaos from a confusion of generations. The existence of this kind of reaction is perhaps demonstrated by the fact that there seems to be little or no disquiet over the liberty of adoptive brothers and sisters to marry (or, nowadays, brothers- and sisters-in-law) whereas the idea of step-parent and step-child (no closer a relationship in blood) causes concern. We respected such feelings, but wondered whether they were really valid as a basis for a legal prohibition on certain categories of marriage. People, who in kinship terms might not be expected to be of different 'generations', may in practice be of much the same age (as in some of the cases covered by the Personal Bills). Furthermore, the law already tolerates marriage between people who may be of very different ages (including those who may have some affinal or kinship link such as brothers- and sisters-in-law). It is possible that marriage between people of very different ages may continue to be distasteful to some – and in some cases ill-advised – but there is no reason for the law (with the exception already mentioned to protect a 'child of the family') to prohibit such marriages.

111.   Secondly, it was argued that abolition of the existing impediments might have a significant effect on the number of marriages solemnised, and the number of primary family groups formed, and the institution of the family would be undermined merely to satisfy the pursuit of individualism. We do not accept this argument. It is not possible to estimate how many couples might take advantage of the liberty in law and marry if the existing impediments were removed. The number of persons who may be related by affinity has grown enormously as a result of the increase in the number of marriages, and of divorces and second marriages. But there has not been any sustained pressure or demand from the general public for a change in the law and therefore we have presumed that the number of such hidden couples will be very small though they may increase in the future with the increasing number of remarriages (see Chapter 8).

112.   Thirdly it has been suggested that public opinion is not ready for changes in the present restrictions, and that any such change might result in a feeling of repugnance or anxiety when what some might consider (by analogy) 'incestuous' relationships were to be permitted by the general law.

113.   The likelihood of some such reaction is something which it is not easy to measure. Public opinion on the possible changes has not in fact been tested. Certainly flamboyant articles appear in the popular press from time to time presenting colourful stories about sex or marriage between step-relations (as on other sexual topics), but the general goodwill and lack of scandal which seemed to have accompanied the Personal Bills suggests that public opinion may be more open than is sometimes assumed. Three lawful marriages within the prohibited degrees have now been contracted (following the passing of the Personal Bills by Parliament) without any outrage apparently being felt by the general public.

114.   Some pointers may be taken from the history of the last enactment in this area, the *Marriage (Enabling) Act 1960*. This extended to a divorced wife's sister the right to marry which in 1907 had been given to a deceased wife's sister. The 1960 Act was debated only once, on Second Reading in the House of Lords. All other stages in the House of Lords, and all stages in the House of Commons, passed without debate. In the House of Lords the Bill was opposed by the Archbishop of Canterbury (Lord Fisher) and the Bishop of Lichfield (Dr A. S. Reeve). Both spoke of revulsion, but used the term about the simple adultery (not marriage) of a husband with his wife's sister, and also about the use of such adultery as an unjust and cruel pressure exercised upon a wife to divorce her husband, so freeing him to marry her sister. There was only one other speech against the Bill. Another speaker was the Bishop of Exeter at the time (Dr R. C. Mortimer – himself the leading episcopal authority on moral theology and the canon law) but he did not declare himself against the Bill. In the end, the Bill passed without a division, though three Bishops were present.

115. In proposing the Bill Lord Mancroft recalled a previous and unsuccessful Bill of 1949. On that occasion the Bishop of Winchester (Dr Haigh) supported the Bill, and recalled the grave misgivings which had surrounded the *Deceased Wife's Sister Act 1907*, including the fears of Archbishop Davidson. Such had been the unease that the 1907 Act had been before the House of Lords on no fewer than nineteen occasions before it was passed. In the event the fears and misgivings had proved to be unfounded.

116. It must be right to mention that the *Marriage (Enabling) Act 1960* was passed nine years before the *Divorce Reform Act 1969* which substantially reformed the law of divorce. Since 1969 the sole ground for divorce is that the marriage has broken down irretrievably; this may be established by one of several facts including the fact that the parties to the marriage have lived apart for a continuous period of at least five years. A petition for divorce based on this fact, if proved, enables a marriage to be dissolved against the wishes of the respondent.[11] Furthermore the number of marriages dissolved since the law of divorce has been reformed has increased dramatically.

117. The Group considered whether these matters affect the issue of public opinion. The general view of the majority of us is that, with the safeguards we suggest and on the clear understanding that only affines and not consanguineous relations are affected, such changes as we propose may well find relatively easy acceptance.

118. In conclusion, the only argument in support of the existing legal impediments that carried substantial weight with us concerned the risk to younger members of the primary family. Applying this conclusion to the present law the relationships of step-parent and step-child are in practice the only degrees which are likely to need protection. We decided that no other arguments we had heard outweighed the general principle of the right or liberty to marry.

---

[11]An examination of the statistics shows that the number of petitions based on this fact declined by a quarter between 1978 and 1981 inclusive.

## Arguments for Abolishing the Existing Impediments

119.  There is undoubtedly logical force in the various abolitionist arguments. They are based largely on the principle that marriage is a presumed liberty, restraints upon which require specific justification. Thus restrictions on the liberty of two individuals to marry which are no longer valid or necessary today should be removed. We agree with this general statement but recognise that other considerations also affect family relationships.

### FREEDOM TO MARRY

120.  In considering the question of the civil law of marriage the initial position from which to begin is one of fundamental freedom to marry. Such a freedom is buttressed from several directions. The *European Convention for the Protection of Human Rights and Freedoms* stands in a long tradition of enlightened rationalism. Its Article 12 says:

> Men and women of marriageable age have the right to marry and to found a family, according to the national laws governing the exercise of this right.

The juristic traditions of most European states do not speak of *granting a right* so much as of *recognising a freedom* to marry, going on perhaps to *regulate* that freedom in the interest of spouses in a particular marriage, or with the aim of protecting the institution of marriage from assault from one quarter or another.

121.  The Christian tradition also emphasises the freedom to marry, though it does so from its own particular reasoning. It turns to Jesus's argument (when questioned about divorce) that sexuality and marriage is a divine ordinance (as eating and working are) consistent with man's nature. Jesus implies that the perfection of marriage is sufficiently declared in the passage in Genesis 2 which narrates the original institution of the holy estate of matrimony at the creation (Matthew 19 or Mark 10). 'The teaching and legislation of the Christian Church on this subject may, therefore, from one point of view, be regarded as

a series of attempts to define more clearly and fully what is implied in the words of the original institution, and to enforce in practice the careful observance of the principles therein involved' (W. M. Foley in *Encyclopedia of Religion and Ethics*). Hence the brevity of the New Testament treatment of marriage – on one level it was taken for granted, and at another it provided the typology for describing Christ's relationship with his church. St Paul – a pharisee of the pharisees – derived his liberty to marry, like his liberty to eat and drink, from the fundamental freedom given to him by his Creator.

122.   It is this basic freedom, however we derive it, that the civil law is in our opinion concerned to establish, to preserve and protect, rather than to enforce or to underpin the particular marriage disciplines of any one religious group or another. We do not feel it necessary therefore to come to any view or conclusion upon theological or religious considerations put forward (for instance the authority of the Mosaic texts or the doctrine of one flesh) except insofar as they bear upon the nature of marriage, and why the freedom to marry is to be regarded as a natural right.

123.   However, for the law simply to enshrine the freedom to marry *per se* is not enough. In several areas the law puts restraint upon individual liberty, recognising that it may give rise to rivalries with other individuals. Even when that consideration does not seem to arise there may still be limitations, for instance with the intention of protecting people from possibly damaging consequences of the exercise of liberty. For example, young people are not held capable of entering into some civil contracts. They may be restrained from engaging in activities which are thought to be injurious to the health of bodies not yet fully framed into adulthood. Of special interest to us, young people may be protected from some particular aspects of sexual relationship, with the same supposition that they are not yet 'ready' for them, though one day it is expected that they will be. In such cases what seems to be operating is a social pressure, enshrined in laws, to postpone the exercise of a freedom until a time when it may eventually

47

be fully taken up. Beyond this, the law does restrain even a mature adult's freedom to engage in pursuits which society deems to be damaging to the individual concerned. Thus, gaming contracts, and contracts to suffer physical pain, will not be enforced at law. In these two circumstances (where freedoms are in conflict, or where particular kinds of harm may come to the person exercising his freedom, or to society itself), the law may impose restrictions. We accept the principle that such statutory restrictions may be justified in particular circumstances.

### RECENT HISTORY

124.   Whatever arguments from theology or doctrine may govern the canon law of the Church of England or the individual disciplines of other religious bodies, we accept that for the purposes of the general law the prohibited degrees of affinity constitute a restriction which has to be justified on more general grounds and substantiated by cogent reasons. As we have seen, history shows that in practice there has been considerable legislative freedom in this field. Before the *Marriage Act 1835* a marriage between persons within the 'prohibited degrees'[12] was voidable (and therefore prima facie valid) by decree of an ecclesiastical court pronounced during the lifetime of both parties. Since 1835 such marriages have been void (i.e. void *ab initio*). The four statutes earlier this century significantly changed the law of affinity by removing 20 degrees (total for man and woman) from the list of prohibited degrees. The relationships removed included one's brother-in-law or sister-in-law (which constitute for many

[12]The expression 'prohibited degrees' was not defined in the *Marriage Act 1835* but it was interpreted in the case of *R v. Chadwick* (1847). The Court of Queen's Bench refused to be drawn into a consideration of Hebrew marriage law but took the view that 'God's Law', the 'levitical degrees' and the 'prohibited degrees' must mean the degrees within which a marriage would have been subject to annulment by the ecclesiastical courts before 1835; Lord Chief Justice Denman expressly referred to Archbishop Parker's Table. The Court's approach in Chadwick's case was approved by the House of Lords in *Brook v. Brook* (1861).

people the nearest affine relative outside the primary family) as well as one's uncle or aunt and nephew or niece (where there is no consanguineous relationship). Together these statutes made significant inroads into the original list of prohibited degrees drawn up by Archbishop Parker, and the changes thus made are virtually universally accepted. Those in favour of abolition argued that there is no good reason for retaining the remaining prohibited degrees, many of which are more distant from the primary family than those removed earlier this century. Pressure to make further changes ought not to come as a surprise, nor can it be regarded prima facie as misconceived: the Private Members' bills introduced by Lady Wootton and Lord Lloyd are examples of that pressure.

125. We recognise the strength of this argument but conclude that legislative neatness alone is not a sufficient reason to promote important social reforms in the face of objections from several quarters of informed opinion, and warnings on social and/or psychological grounds that abolition of the impediments might bring some dangers and difficulties. But where it seems impossible for the younger person during his or her minority ever to have been in the same family or household as the older person – and this is the case in several of the degrees of in-law relationships at present included in Schedule 1 of the *Marriage Act 1949* (see class D in paragraphs 206 and 221f) – there cannot be the same concern for the younger person wishing to marry his or her elder affine.

THE EXPERIENCE OF OTHER STATES

126. We took careful note that in some other states lawful impediments against marriages between affines have never existed, and that other states have abolished them with no obvious damage to their family structure or to the fabric of their society (see Chapter 7). However, simple comparisons with the law of other states may be unsafe. In states whose legal systems have never prescribed impediments against marriage between affines other influences or constraints in their society or cultures may be of influence. For example, in non-western

or non-Christian societies the incest taboo often extends in directions different from those which in this country are commonly considered to be its boundaries. Sometimes sexual relationships between some (though not all) affines are prohibited. Comparisons with countries which have abolished earlier impediments are difficult to make. Some have abolished the impediments but evidence of the effects (if any) of abolition on the family structure or fabric of the society does not seem to have been scientifically assessed; we have not been made aware, in fact, that such studies have been made.

## PERSONAL BILL PROCEDURE AND POSSIBLE ALTERNATIVE PROCEDURES

127.   The unsatisfactory nature of the Personal Bill procedure has already been discussed (paras 41–46). Some representations submitted that a suitable and satisfactory alternative procedure cannot be devised and it would be best to abolish the legal impediment altogether rather than continue to prohibit couples related by affinity from marrying. They suggest that the issue of whether or not two people may marry is not one with which the law should concern itself and therefore a court procedure would not be suitable whilst an administrative procedure would not be reviewable.

128.   We are not persuaded by this argument; we believe that a suitable administrative or administrative and judical procedure can be devised, and a suggested outline is given later (Chapter 11).

## UNHAPPINESS CAUSED BY THE EXISTING LAW

129.   Finally we considered the position of a couple related by affinity who wish to marry but are not allowed to do so under the present law. We have no information how many such couples there are, but one may presume that some have decided to live together as husband and wife. Today there is less social stigma attached to an unmarried couple cohabiting than there was even only ten years ago. One unfortunate and unhappy result in the present law is that, if a couple cohabit as husband

and wife and cannot marry because they are related within the existing prohibited degrees, their children, if any, must remain illegitimate in law. Whilst illegitimacy is less stigmatised today, there are a number of residual disadvantages for a person who is illegitimate compared with a person born in wedlock. In spite of the high number of divorces and the trauma which children often suffer when marriage breaks down, the wish to marry remains strong. Freedom to marry should be restricted in as few cases as possible.

130. In conclusion, we found the arguments of the abolitionists generally persuasive and acknowledged that the individual's freedom to marry ought to be bound or tied by few legal restrictions or limitations. However, we agreed that even this important freedom of the individual may be limited or defined by law, where the restriction protects either the individual or the institution of marriage for the benefit of all persons in the land. The minimum age of marriage and the minimum age of consent are examples of restrictions for the protection of the individual, and the principle of monogamy and the requirements of notice, public ceremony and registration are examples of the law defining, dignifying and strengthening the institution of marriage.

# CHAPTER SEVEN
## The Law and Practice in Other States

131. Before drawing its conclusions and deciding upon its recommendations the Group considered the law and practice of a number of other States, as expressly required by its terms of reference. Most interesting for this purpose are those legal systems which stem from the common law of this country and serve populations containing a strong English-speaking element. Other traditions of interest are those of our European neighbours.

## English-Speaking Countries

132. In the *United States of America* there are great variations in the laws of affinity between states. For instance, in Georgia and Mississippi marriages between step-parents and children are criminal offences of 'incest' carrying terms of up to three years' imprisonment. In 24 mostly western, northern and central states marriages between step-parents and children are permitted, while in 22 mostly eastern and southern states these are forbidden.

133. In the earlier-settled East and South where assumptions and precedents drawn from religious teaching had influenced civil lawmaking, the impediments included affinal as well as consanguineous relationships, but in the Western states, with laws that were more recently formulated, there was less attempt to introduce religious precepts into the civil law and affinal impediments are absent.

134. States which prohibit marriage between step-parents and step-children generally prohibit also marriage between in-laws, though there is considerable variation as to which in-law relationships are included in the prohibitions.

135. The law of *Canada* prohibits the solemnization of matrimony between step-parents and step-children. Similarly a person may not marry his son's wife or her daughter's husband. Exceptions can be made in individual cases by private Act of Parliament.

136. In *New Zealand*, courts have attempted to distinguish cases in which a general impediment to the marriage of affines might be relaxed. In *Australia* too, prior to 1975, similar considerations of such relaxations are to be found. A number of our correspondents favoured the importation of some similar procedures into our own law. That is not our opinion, and we state the reasons for our disagreement in Chapter 9, but in arriving at our view we looked closely at the New Zealand and Australian experience.

137. In *New Zealand* there are legal impediments to the marriage of affines but a court of law may dispense a couple from the impediment. Section 15 of the *Marriage Act 1955*[13] provides inter alia:

> (2) Any persons who are not within the degrees of consanguinity but are within the degrees of affinity . . . may apply to the Supreme Court for its consent to their marriage, and the Court, if it is satisfied that neither party to the intended marriage has by his or her conduct caused or contributed to the cause of the termination of any previous marriage of the other party, may make an order dispensing with the prohibition . . . so far as it relates to the parties to the application and, if such an order is made, that prohibition shall cease to apply to the parties.

138. Adopted children are legally within the degrees of consanguinity, and therefore cannot apply for dispensation. Applicants to the Supreme Court may be cross-examined, and the Solicitor-General in the two reported cases[14] acted for the

---

[13]Consolidated in *Matrimonial Proceedings Act 1963* section 7
[14]*In Re Woodcock and Woodcock* (1957) NZLR 960-986
 *In Re Hoskin and Pearson* (1958 NZLR) 605-608

Court as independent counsel. If the conditions of Section 15 are fulfilled the dispensation is not automatic. The Court does not consider itself bound to dispense with the relevant prohibition. Its discretion is unfettered – it does not act, as it were, as a rubber stamp – and it is not possible for a set of general principles to be laid down. However, judges have taken the view that where the step-child has known the step-parent as a parent and grown up in the same family, it is less desirable for the parties to marry, than with applicants who have never known each other in a parent-child role. The manner of the dissolution of the former marriage of the other party is, under the statute, crucial. If one applicant is found by the Court to have contributed to or caused the termination of any previous marriage of the other party, the Court has no discretion in the matter and it cannot dispense the couple from the legal impediment.

139.    The first case under the section to be reported is *In Re Woodcock and Woodcock* (1957) in the Court of Appeal. The judge at first instance was seeking guidance in interpreting the meaning of the 'satisfaction' which the section required him to arrive at before issuing a dispensation to a step-father and a step-daughter to permit them to marry. The parties did not appear. The Court of Appeal remitted the case for determination of the facts with a direction that the Court should seek the assistance of the Solicitor-General in the role of *amicus curiae*, since otherwise there is no opposing party to an application for such a dispensation. It was noted that the only parallel jurisdiction from which example might be taken was that of Tasmania. The direction made by the Court of Appeal with regard to the nature of the satisfaction necessary was a technical one, but it was not of the level of being 'beyond reasonable doubt'. That is the test of proof in a criminal case. What was required was an appearance that no conduct of the applicants was a cause of termination of an earlier marriage. After the determination of the matter of conduct, the discretion of the Court remained because the Act is permissive, and not mandatory, about the issue of a dispensation. The decision of

the Supreme Court when it reconsidered the case is not reported.

140.   The other reported case was *In Re Hoskin and Pearson* (1958) in the Supreme Court. The Court required the applicants to give oral evidence and to be cross-examined by counsel for the Solicitor-General, appearing as *amicus curiae*. The judge then declared himself 'fully satisfied' that neither applicant was 'in any way responsible for, or a factor in or related to, the termination of earlier marriages'. The application for a dispensation still remained in the Court's discretion. In the absence of any guidance either from the statute or from the Court of Appeal, the judge took into account these considerations:

> the realities (as opposed to the legalities) of the relationship of the applicants: were they of the nature of guardian and ward; had the step-father in age and practical matters and aspect stood in something like a true father's position: the answers to these questions would help in solving the next consideration;

> the likely reaction of public opinion when the details become known – would it be likely to be one of abhorrence?

> the best interests of public morality;

> the presence or absence of ulterior motives, such as material gain;

> the consequences of the birth of children – would children create difficulties or prejudice to existing families or children?

> there were other possible considerations.

On the facts the judge found in favour of the applicants and granted them dispensation.

141.   *Australia* provides an interesting example of a country whose law of affinity has undergone development in recent times.

142.   The *Matrimonial Causes Act 1959* followed the approach

of the Tasmanian and New Zealand law. Section 20 provided *inter alia*:

> (1) Where two persons who are within the prohibited degrees of affinity wish to marry one another, they may apply in writing to a judge for permission to do so.
>
> (2) If the Judge is satisfied that the circumstances of the particular case are so exceptional as to justify the granting of the permission sought, he may, by order, permit the applicants to marry one another.

143.    There is one reported case involving the interpretation of this section. In *Re an application by P and P* (1973)[15] Mr Justice Crockett in the Supreme Court of Victoria was able to draw on the New Zealand analogies in making up his mind whether the facts that he had before him could be regarded as 'so exceptional', and, if they could be so regarded, how he should exercise his consequent discretion. He found it a difficult case. In the first place he found himself exercising an administrative rather than a judicial function, and subject therefore to no appeal. Not exercising a judicial function he had no power to ask the Attorney-General to intervene and assist him as *amicus curiae* and instead had to rely on affidavits presented to him. In considering what circumstances might be regarded as 'so exceptional' the matter became subjective to the particular applicants – no catalogue of circumstances that are or are not capable of being exceptional could be given and no attempt to define them exhaustively ought to be undertaken. Each case needed to be looked at in the light of its own particular merits. The judge tried to resort to what were believed to be current community beliefs and standards – social, moral, ethical and religious – and observed that the task of determining these standards and beliefs had never been more difficult, though he did not feel that society was then so 'spiritually sterile' as to permit the complete abolition of the impediment (though it was so abolished by statute two years later).

144.    The judge, without attempting to be exhaustive, listed

---

[15] 1973 VR 533

the following as factors likely to produce a reaction of repugnance in people generally who heard about them:

substantial disparity in the ages of the applicants;

the closeness of the relationship;

whether either applicant had children, and if so, their ages;

the relationship of the other parent of any such children to the other applicant;

the attitude of such parent to the proposed marriage;

the competition for the affection of such children that might be created by the marriage's taking place;

any risk of the impairment of such children's future happiness and welfare to which they might be exposed by the contemplated marriage's taking place;

whether either of the applicants had by his or her conduct caused or contributed to the termination of any previous marriage of the other party;

whether the intended marriage was desired for an unworthy reason on the part of one applicant such as the possession of a predatory motive;

whether the applicants had begotten children who might be legitimated by the intended marriage's taking place;

the circumstances of any past relationship between the applicants such as a step-daughter having been reared from an early age by a step-father as though his natural child or the parties standing in the relationship of guardian and ward.

145. Two unreported cases showed how 'oppressed' judges felt at having to decide what circumstances might be unexceptional so as to indicate what, by comparison, might be exceptional. In the case before him, Mr Justice Crockett found that the supplanting of the former husband by his own father (the case concerned the question of the marriage of a father-in-law and his daughter-in-law), and the position of children of the former marriage (whose grandfather would now become also their stepfather, and whose step-brother or sister would be a child of their grandfather), together constituted a degree of 'unseemliness' and so he refused permission. Reviewing the case in a learned journal, one writer

comments that the decision hinged on the judge's estimate of the importance of the considerations he listed rather than upon exceptionality, which was what the statute directed.

146.    If a parent-in-law and a child-in-law in Australia wish to marry now they are free in law to do so. As a result of the *Family Law Act 1975* there are few prohibited degrees. Prohibition now applies only to ancestors and descendants and to brothers and sisters (whether of the whole blood or the half blood).

147.    We received conflicting statements about the way the *Family Law Act 1975* has been received. The change itself originated in the Senate of the Australian Federal Parliament and was debated only briefly in the House of Representatives, though the division at the Committee stage was carried by a proportion of only four to three. The Chief Judge of the Family Court of Australia, Mrs Justice Evatt, informed the Group that the abolition of the impediments of affinity had been simply a matter of rationalisation of the law. She further stated that there had been no public concern or opposition to abolition from sociologists or psychologists either at the time the law was changed or in the seven years since 1975.

148.    On the other hand, after the *Family Law Act 1975* had become law, the Anglican Church in Australia perceived important differences between what was permitted by the general law and the traditional requirements of the Canon Law (of their Church). The Archbishop of Adelaide, the Most Rev. Keith Rayner, wrote to a member of the Group and described the difference as a 'great gulf'. For historical reasons the Canon Law varied from diocese to diocese. The national Church was anxious to enact one pattern in the field of prohibited relationships but was reluctant to adopt the same reforms which had been made in the general law without further investigation. The General Synod of Australia saw considerable danger in the widening of the possibilities of marriage permitted by civil legislation and the minimal nature of the Table of Prohibited Degrees in the current civil legislation

as a serious threat to the integrity of family life. As an interim measure, therefore, the General Synod passed in 1981 a new Canon, Canon C15, for adoption by each diocese. The new Canon is in the same terms as Canon B31 of the Church of England (para 21).

149.   Neither the Chief Judge nor the Archbishop informed us of any actual marriages contracted as a result of the abolition of the impediments in 1975; there may not have been any such marriages. We do know that in thirteen of the fourteen years during which the *Matrimonial Causes Act 1959* was in operation a total of only 22 decrees of nullity were made on all grounds including consanguinity, affinity, place of celebration, and that small total needs to be seen alongside the much larger figure of 10,000 or 15,000 divorce decrees per year.


## Some European Countries

150.   Brief details follow of the marriage law as it affects affines in most Western European countries and some relevant procedural provisions. The Group has relied for this section largely upon an information paper compiled by the Council of Europe in response to another enquiry. More detailed correspondence by our secretaries helped us with the cases of Finland, the Republic of Ireland, the Soviet Union and Spain. Without more study than we were able to undertake it has been impossible to harmonise the terminology used in these reports with our own. We have therefore simply reproduced the language of the information paper, and append a note about the definitions used in it.

151.   On the information available to the Group it is difficult to make reliable comparisons between any two European countries or parallels for our own situation, or to make objective comment. Many of the statements refer to exceptions or dispensations being made from a particular rule, without making clear what circumstances are considered, and how often requests for such exceptions are either made or granted.

Fuller information has been received from Austria, Denmark, France, Iceland, Norway and West Germany, and it is set out in the Table on pages 66 and 67.

## 152. AUSTRIA
Marriage is prohibited between persons related by affinity in the direct line, whether or not legitimate, even if the marriage from which the affinity originated has been declared void or terminated. However, this prohibition may be waived for serious reasons.

## 153. BELGIUM
(a) Marriage is prohibited between ascendants and descendants related by affinity in the direct line, whether or not legitimate.
(b) Marriage is prohibited between persons related by affinity in the collateral line up to the second degree. However, affinity in this context does not constitute an obstacle to marriage if the person who created the affinity has died.
If the marriage from which the affinity originated was terminated by divorce a dispensation may be granted for serious reasons.

## 154. CYPRUS
In Cyprus, the prohibitions of marriage between persons of the Greek Community are governed by the autocephalous Church of Cyprus. Muslim Law governs the family relations between persons of the Turkish Community in the island.

## 155. DENMARK
Marriage is prohibited between a person and the ascendant or descendant in the direct line, or his or her former spouse, unless the Minister of Justice grants permission by Decree. If there are common children by the former marriage, such permission may only be granted if the welfare of the children is not prejudiced thereby.

## 156. FRANCE

(a) Marriage is prohibited between ascendants and descendants, whether or not legitimate, related by affinity in the direct line. However, a dispensation may be granted for serious reasons if the person who created the affinity has died.

(b) Marriage is also prohibited between persons related by affinity in the collateral line up to the second degree, if the marriage which created the affinity was terminated by divorce. However, a dispensation may be granted for serious reasons.

## 157. FEDERAL REPUBLIC OF GERMANY

Marriage is prohibited between persons related by affinity in the direct line. This prohibition may be waived unless there are serious reasons why such a marriage should not take place. Until 1970 such marriages were treated as incestuous and carried penalties of two years' imprisonment. Support is building up for the total abolition of the prohibition of marriage between persons related by marriage, but there is no information of when legislation might be introduced.

## 158. FINLAND

(a) Marriage with ascendants or descendants of a spouse (including step-parents or children) is prohibited.

(b) Marriage between brother and sister, and their descendants, is prohibited.

(c) Marriage is prohibited where there has formerly been a marriage to an ascendant or descendant relative of the proposed spouse (e.g. parents-in-law or child-in-law). This prohibition may be dispensed by the President of the Republic for 'particularly strong reasons', defined as including cases where the parties are ignorant of the impediment, or have never enjoyed a close family relationship.

(d) Information received does not distinguish between former marriages terminated by death and those dissolved by divorce.

(e) Legislation is now going through the Finnish parliament which would offer some alleviation of the above prohibitions.

The draft legislation is intended to enable cases under (a) to be dispensed by the Minister of Justice where there are strong reasons. Marriages with brother's or sister's descendants (see (b)) would be rather more easily dispensed. If the draft legislation becomes law the ban on cases under (c) would be totally removed.

(f) There are other prohibitions concerning adoptive or fiduciary relationships which do not concern our subject.

### 159. GREECE

Marriage is prohibited between persons related by affinity in the direct line indefinitely or in the collateral line up to the third degree.

### 160. ICELAND

Marriage is prohibited between a person and the ascendant or descendant in the direct line of his or her former spouse, unless the Ministry of Justice grants permission by decree.

### 161. REPUBLIC OF IRELAND

In Ireland the list of prohibited degrees is different from ours. All the degrees which we prohibit are prohibited there and they prohibit also marriages with uncle's wife and aunt's husband, nephew's wife and niece's husband and wife's niece and husband's nephew. There is no judical or administrative procedure to obtain a dispensation from the prohibitions, though one could be obtained by a procedure analogous to our parliamentary personal bill process. The Roman Catholic church does make dispensations for marriages contracted within the prohibited degrees but such marriages performed in Ireland would be null and void at civil law.

### 162. ITALY

(a) Marriage is prohibited between persons related by affinity in the direct line; this prohibition also applies where the marriage which creates the affinity is declared void, where it has been terminated or where a court has declared that it shall no longer give rise to civil effects. Dispensation may be granted only when the affinity originates from a marriage which has been declared void.

(b) Marriage is prohibited between persons related by affinity in the collateral line up to the second degree. Dispensation may be granted for serious reasons.

### 163. LUXEMBOURG

(a) Marriage is prohibited between ascendants or descendants related by affinity in the direct line, whether or not legitimate.

(b) Marriage is prohibited between persons related by affinity in the collateral line up to the second degree.

### 164. MALTA

Marriage is prohibited between persons related by affinity in the direct line.

### 165. NETHERLANDS

Marriage is prohibited between ascendants and descendants related by affinity in the direct line.

### 166. NORWAY

Marriage is prohibited between a person and the ascendant and descendant in the direct line of his or her former spouse unless permission is granted by Royal Decree. If there are common children by the former marriage, such permission is only granted if the welfare of the children is not prejudiced thereby.

### 167. PORTUGAL

Marriage is prohibited between persons related by affinity in the direct line.

## 168. SOVIET UNION

(a) Marriage is prohibited between relatives in direct line of ascendance or descendance, between full or half-brothers or sisters, and also between adoptive and adopted persons, unless the adoption be legally dissolved.

(b) Step-relations may marry, as may cousins, aunt and nephew and uncle and niece.

## 169. SPAIN

(a) Marriage is prohibited between ascendants and descendants related by affinity in the direct line, whether or not legitimate.

(b) Marriage is prohibited between persons related by legitimate affinity in the collateral line up to the fourth degree.

(c) Marriage is prohibited between persons related by illegitimate affinity in a collateral line up to the second degree.

In cases under (b) and (c) above the competent authorities may, for serious reasons, grant a dispensation.

## 170. SWEDEN

No prohibition of marriage between persons related by affinity.

## 171. SWITZERLAND

Marriage is prohibited between persons related by affinity in the direct line; this provision also applies in the event that the marriage from which the affinity originated is declared void or terminated by death or divorce.

## 172. TURKEY

Marriage is prohibited between persons related by affinity in the direct line; this provision also applies in the event that the marriage from which the affinity originated is declared void or terminated by death or divorce.

*Note to the above statements* (see paragraph 150)

173. The term 'line' indicates the link between the members of a family. Such a link may be 'direct' or 'collateral'. Affinity

'in the direct line' refers to the descendants and ascendants of the spouse e.g. son-in-law and mother-in-law, daughter-in-law and father-in-law. Affinity in the direct line also refers to the link established between a person and the children born of a previous marriage of his or her spouse, whether or not this person is widowed or divorced, e.g. step-daughter and step-father, step-son and step-mother. Affinity 'in the collateral line' refers to those relations of the spouse who descend from the same progenitor. As to the 'degrees' in the collateral line, brother-in-law and sister-in-law are of the second degree, uncle and niece, and aunt and nephew are of the third degree.

SUMMARY OF THE POSITION IN EUROPE

174. Thus, the following countries in Europe appear to maintain a total prohibition against the types of marriage which concern us:

> Cyprus, Finland (as to step-relations), Greece, Republic of Ireland, Luxembourg, Malta, Netherlands, Portugal, Spain (close relations), Switzerland and Turkey.

175. The following countries maintain a general prohibition but admit of some dispensation (the ease or difficulty with which dispensations may be obtained is not known to the Group):

> Austria, Belgium, Denmark, France, West Germany, Finland (as to in-laws), Iceland, Italy, Norway and Spain (distant relations).

176. The following countries have no prohibitions at all:

> Soviet Union, Sweden.

177. The following countries are considering abolishing their present prohibitions:

> Finland (as to in-laws), West Germany.

178. The Table on pages 66 and 67 details the results of a questionnaire which the Home Office sent to the British embassies in six European countries which provide for dispensation. They throw a little more light upon the circumstances surrounding the process of permitting and granting dispensations. The terminology here is not our own.

*Table to paragraphs 151 and 178: Summary of procedures in six West European countries for the granting of permission to affines to marry*

| | AUSTRIA | DENMARK |
|---|---|---|
| (1) Is the application for a dispensation from the general legal prohibition made to a court or to an administrative organ within Government? | Administrative (but with court involvement) | Administrative |
| (2) Is provision made for others who may be concerned to be told about the application and do such persons have an opportunity to support or to oppose the application? | No provision in existing legislation for others to be told | Other persons concerned are notified and questioned if judged appropriate, and their views taken into account in suitable cases |
| (3) Are the criteria for the consideration of such applications publicly known, whether or not embodied in legal provisions? What are they? | Yes, i.e. the First Regulation of 27 July 1983 of the German law on marriage | Under s7 of Marriage Law 256 of 1969, authorisation is only granted if the marriage does not run counter to best interests of children of previous marriage. Weight is given to the existence of any parent–child relationship between the applicants and whether their relationship contributed to the dissolution of the previous marriage |
| (4) In what way (if at all) is the existence of children of the former marriage(s) of the applicant relevant to the determination of an application to marry a step–child? | All relevant factors must be taken into account | The Marriage Law states that regard for the best interests of the children of the impediment-producing previous marriage must be paramount. Little importance is attached to whether applicants have other children |
| (5) Is the manner of the dissolution of the former marriage(s) i.e. whether it was by death or divorce (whether or not involving either of the applicants) material in granting or withholding a dispensation? | The previous marriage must have been dissolved at least one year previously. The man must not be much younger than the woman | How the former marriage was ended is significant. If the applicants' relationship contributed to the dissolution of the previous marriage by divorce a dispensation may be withheld. |
| (6) How are the costs of an application, and of any necessary enquiries related to it, borne? | Fees payable by applicant | Costs of application and enquiries borne by public funds |

## Table to paragraphs 151 and 178 (continued)

| | FRANCE | ICELAND | NORWAY | WEST GERMANY |
|---|---|---|---|---|
| | Administrative | Administrative | Administrative | Court |
| | Not specifically, only by publication of bann etc. But third parties are likely to learn of the application by receiving official enquiries and will have an opportunity to oppose it | Only if one of the parties to the intended marriage is under 20 years of age and was not previously married. Parental consent necessary in such cases | Former spouses and children will be invited to give their opinions | Not specifically but others concerned may be approached by the court |
| | Embodied in Civil Code Article 164 Generally known that dispensation is granted only in serious cases | Not embodied in any legal provision. Not publicly known | No set criteria beyond Section 8 of Marriage Act (see below) | s4 Clause 1 of Federal German Marriage Law forbids marriages between step-parents/children. However, the court must under s4 clause 2 grant dispensation in absence of 'important reasons' against |
| | Dispensation probably granted if marriage would improve the position of children of former marriage | Not relevant | Under s8 of the Marriage Act permission only granted if considerations concerning children of former marriages are favourable | Can be a factor against, but not always |
| | No dispensation if previous marriage dissolved by divorce | No | No definite rules but manner of dissolution may be taken into account | Quick succession of marriages may count against |
| | Fee of 500f but waived in suitable cases | Costs borne by applicant(s) | No official fees but may be legal advice costs incurred by the applicants | Fees payable by applicants. No fees if dispensation not granted or application withdrawn |

# CHAPTER EIGHT
## Statistics

### The Size of the Class of People who might be affected by a Change in the Law[16]

179.   The number of people who are related by affinity has grown in recent years. A major trend in marriage is the increasing proportion of marriages which are re-marriage for one or both partners. The increase may be seen by examining the number of marriages for whom for one or both partners the marriage is a second (or later) marriage.

| *Marriages* | Great Britain | | | | | | UK |
|---|---|---|---|---|---|---|---|
| | 1961 | 1971 | 1976 | 1979 | 1980 | 1981 | 1981 |
| Marriages (thousands) | | | | | | | |
| 1st marriage for both parents | 331 | 357 | 273 | 270 | 270 | 255 | 263 |
| 1st marriage for one partner only | | | | | | | |
| Bachelor/divorced woman | 11 | 21 | 30 | 33 | 33 | 31 | 32 |
| Bachelor/widow | 5 | 4 | 3 | 3 | 3 | 3 | 3 |
| Spinster/divorced man | 12 | 24 | 32 | 36 | 37 | 36 | 36 |
| Spinster/widower | 8 | 5 | 4 | 3 | 3 | 3 | 3 |
| 2nd (or later) marriage for both partners | | | | | | | |
| Both divorced | 5 | 17 | 34 | 43 | 45 | 44 | 44 |
| Both widowed | 10 | 10 | 9 | 8 | 8 | 7 | 7 |
| Divorced man/widow | 3 | 4 | 5 | 5 | 5 | 5 | 5 |
| Divorced woman/widower | 3 | 5 | 5 | 5 | 5 | 5 | 5 |
| Total marriages | 387 | 447 | 396 | 407 | 409 | 388 | 398 |
| remarriages* as a percentage of all marriages | 15 | 20 | 31 | 34 | 34 | 34 | 34 |

*Remarriage for one or both partners

---

[16]The Group was much assisted by a written submission from the *Family Policy Studies Centre* (formerly known as the Study Commission on the Family), 3 Park Road, London and this Chapter is based on that evidence. The tables are extracted from information published by the *Office of Population Censuses and Surveys*, the *General Register Office (Scotland)* and the *General Register Office (Northern Ireland)*.

In 1981 66 per cent of all marriages involved first marriages for both parties and 19 per cent for one spouse only; in the remaining 16 per cent of marriages both partners had previously been married.

180.   The increase in the proportion of marriages for which the marriage is a second (or later) marriage for one or both partners reflects the increase in divorce in recent years.

*Divorces*

| | 1961 | 1971 | 1976 | 1979 | 1980 | 1981 | 1982 |
|---|---|---|---|---|---|---|---|
| England and Wales Decrees absolute granted (thousands) | 25 | 74 | 127 | 138 | 148 | 146 | 147 |
| United Kingdom Total divorces granted (thousands) | 27 | 80 | 136 | 148 | 160 | 157 | 159 |
| Percentage of divorces where one or both partners had been divorced previously England and Wales | 9.3 | 8.8 | 11.6 | 14.7 | 15.7 | 17.1 | 18.5 |

181.   In each subsequent marriage a new set of affines is acquired. Step-relationships increase; children acquire step-parents and may acquire step-grandparents; and parents of remarried spouses may acquire step-grandchildren. The marrying partners acquire parents-in-law where their spouse's parents are living.

182.   The whole issue of the extensiveness of step-relationships is under-researched. Given the increase in divorce the number of children whose parents re-marry directly relates to the number of step-relationships. The following Table shows the number of children involved in divorces in England and Wales.

*Number and ages of children stated to be under 16 of couples divorced in England and Wales*

| | 0-4 | 5-10 | 11-15 | Total |
|---|---|---|---|---|
| 1970 | 18,837 | 34,996 | 17,503 | 71,336 |
| 1975 | 33,372 | 68,678 | 43,046 | 145,096 |
| 1980 | 39,499 | 71,446 | 52,276 | 163,221 |
| 1981 | 40,281 | 67,582 | 51,540 | 159,403 |

183. The average number of children per divorcing couple however has stayed remarkably constant. Thus the fact that more children have been affected simply reflects the increase in the number of divorces. At the current level of divorce one child in five can expect to see their parents divorced before they turn 16. If the number of children should remain the same 1.6 million children would see their parents divorced over the next 10 years. Whether children will have a step-parent will depend on whether one or both of their divorced parents re-marry.

184. For the past 10 years there has been a decline in the total number of marriages (Great Britain 1971: 447,000; 1981: 388,000) with an assumed increase in the number of couples cohabiting. This may result in many relationships analogous to affinity which are not formalised by the marriage of the parents.

185. Of the 146,000 couples who divorced in 1981, 87,000 (60 per cent) had children under the age of 16 and a further 14,000 couples had children over 16. In the majority of cases children remain with their mother after divorce. Thus where a child later has a step-parent on his or her parent remarrying, it is more likely to be a step-father relationship.

186. The General Household Survey 1979 showed that 16 per cent of all children under 16 do not live with both their natural parents: 4 per cent lived with their natural mother and a legal step-father and a further 1 per cent with their natural mother and a cohabitant.

*Children by age and where currently living, Great Britain, 1979*
*Children aged 0-15 of women aged 18-49★*

| Current whereabouts of children | Age of children | | | |
|---|---|---|---|---|
| | 0-4 | 5-9 | 10-15 | Total |
| In the household: | % | % | % | % |
| Living with both natural parents | | | | |
| —married | 88 | 84 | 80 | 83 |
| —cohabiting | 2 | 0 | 0 | 1 |
| natural mother and stepfather | | | | |
| —married | 2 | 4 | 7 | 4 |
| —cohabiting | 1 | 2 | 1 | 1 |
| lone mother | 7 | 9 | 9 | 9 |
| Outside the household: | | | | |
| Living with father (marital status not known) | 0 | 1 | 1 | 1 |
| Adopted or fostered, relatives or non-relatives | 0 | 1 | 1 | 1 |
| At special school or home | 0 | 0 | 1 | 0 |

★Includes 5 married women aged 16 or 17
Source: *General Household Survey 1979*. HMSO. 1981, table 8.23.

## Number of Cases Known to the Group

187.   We should like to have been able to assess accurately the number of couples wishing to marry but who are prevented from doing so because they are related to one another within the prohibited degrees listed in Schedule 1 (as amended) of the *Marriage Act 1949*. But that was beyond practical possibility.[17] So far as we are aware there has been no scientific research done to assess the size of the problem.

188.   Between January 1965 and October 1983 the Home Office and the General Register Office, the two Government departments concerned with the working of the English marriage law, have come to know of 40 cases as the result of receiving written enquiries from couples who wish to marry but who are under the general law unable to do so by reason of affinity. The record kept by these two Government departments does not include telephone enquiries made to either office, or any enquiry made of any superintendent registrar. Most of the cases have concerned step-relations but a handful involved in-laws (Lord Belstead speaking in the House of Lords in the course of the Second Reading debate on the *Marriage (Enabling) Bill [H.L.] 1980/81* gave a figure of 25 cases known then to the Home Office and General Register Office for the 15 year period to February 1981 of which 17 cases involved step-parent or grandstep-parent and step-child and 8 parents-in-law and child-in-law).

189.   Lady Wootton informed us that 11 couples had written to her personally and she wrote to our secretaries as follows:

. . . They come from a wide range of social classes and cover a considerable variety of cases, e.g. step-parent and step-child, father-in-law and daughter-in-law, mother-in-law and son-in-law. They include

---

[17]The *General Register Office* holds no statistical information on the prevalence of couples wishing to marry whose relationship falls within the prohibited degrees of affinity. The *Policy Studies Institute* of 1/2 Castle Street, London has informed the secretaries to the Group that only a population survey would accurately estimate the number of couples who are related by affinity within the terms of Schedule I as amended of the *Marriage Act 1949* and who wish to marry.

divorcees of both sexes, also widows and widowers, and one bachelor and one single girl (not in the same case) . . . Of those who give their ages, several are well on in years (even up to the seventies) and only one (the single girl) is under 20.

. . . The number of my cases is indeed small, but I should think that, if a handful have plucked up the courage to write to a complete stranger, there must be some hundreds in the country as a whole, particularly in view of the variety of situations which they represent. Two or three speak of knowing other couples in similar circumstances . . .

190.    Two couples have written to the Archbishop of Canterbury; in both instances a step-father and step-daughter wish to marry. There were the three couples who brought Personal Bills to Parliament between 1980 and 1982 (see Appendix II) which concerned a step-father wishing to marry his step-daughter in two instances, and in the third instance a step-son wishing to marry his step-mother. Each couple is now married. The solicitor who acted for each of these three couples knows of two other couples wishing to marry; they involve a father-in-law wishing to marry his daughter-in-law and a step-father and step-daughter.

191.    Finally we are aware of two cases which were reported in the press. A case in Manchester involving a step-father and step-daughter received full coverage in the popular press a couple of years ago, and the magazine '*19*' (June 1983) reported a step-daughter wishing to marry her step-father (the latter couple had gone through a form of marriage ceremony in Florida USA).

192.    The total number of cases mentioned is 57 which includes the three couples who brought Personal Bills to Parliament between 1980 and 1982. It is probable that some of these couples will have been in touch with more than one of the persons or offices from whom we have received information in which case one must assume that the figure of 57 includes some double-counting.

193.    It is not possible to assess how many more couples there are who are related by affinity who wish to marry but are prevented from doing so. It is reasonable to suggest that some of them are living together as husband and wife (there is, of

course, no criminal or civil law preventing them from doing so). They may come to terms with their circumstances but presumably not without some anxiety or distress. Other couples may prefer not to live 'in sin' but are equally distressed by their inability to contract a lawful marriage.

194.    We made enquiries of some of the press correspondents commonly called 'agony aunts' who answer family and personal problems of the newspapers' correspondents. The results of these enquiries is interesting. One nationally known 'agony aunt' whose annual mail bag comprises some 50,000 letters estimated that she receives between one and two hundred enquiries every year which are about affinity, and another equally well-known name informed us that she received 'a fairly steady trickle' of enquiries from people about affinity.

# CHAPTER NINE
## Discretion or Criteria?
## Judge, or Superintendent Registrar and Clergyman?

195.   The New Zealand approach – a general prohibition with a provision for a dispensation by a court in appropriate circumstances – has commended itself to some observers, though not, interestingly enough, to many lawyers. The attraction of the New Zealand process seems on closer inspection to be more apparent than real even though it initially provides a clear test for judges to apply: has either party to the intended marriage by his or her conduct caused or contributed to the cause of the termination of any previous marriage of the other party?

196.   The weakness or disadvantage of this approach is that an almost impossible task is placed on the court for two reasons. First, it is now accepted that it is unprofitable to attempt to apportion blame for the breakdown of a marriage. So the concepts of guilt and innocence and of matrimonial offence have disappeared as grounds on which a petition for divorce may be presented. The Courts have strongly discouraged the raising of conduct of the parties as an issue in ancillary financial proceedings. Only in rare and very exceptional cases is it considered relevant. As one of our number perceptively remarked 'The argument may not be about who first threw the rice pudding but rather about how it was cooked.' Conduct is almost always a question of both action and reaction.

197.   Secondly, the New Zealand statutory provision retains for the Court an unfettered discretion whether or not to order a dispensation, even if the Court finds initially that neither party

has by his or her conduct caused or contributed to the cause of termination of any previous marriage. In the Group's view the grant of discretion to the court on a question of whether two people should or should not be permitted to marry places an unreasonable task upon the judge. We have considered the judgments in the two New Zealand reported cases on section 15 of the *Marriage Act 1955* and the Australian case *Re an application by P and P* (1973) (paras 139-145) which drew attention to the difficulty of deciding whether two people should or should not be allowed to marry.

198.  It is not reasonable in the matter of marriage to ask a judge to decide what conduct is acceptable to society at a particular time. Furthermore, the judicial system in this country as in Australia and New Zealand is based on an adversarial approach and here as there it would be necessary to join a law officer of the Crown as *amicus curiae* because for obvious reasons there is no dispute between the two persons who make the application.

199.  Furthermore if the law is changed and if the court is given an unfettered discretion in this matter a body of precedent will not develop. In consequence there would be a lack of certainty in the law, which would be disadvantageous to any persons considering making an application and to their legal advisers.

200.  We have considered whether it is possible to devise a procedure to allow particular couples related by affinity to marry which does not involve discretion, but permits the exception to the general law to be made by reference to unambiguous criteria or guidelines. This approach appeals to us because it would enable the couple to exercise a right which the rest of the population, with few exceptions, enjoys once the applicants have established provable facts to meet the statutory criteria. If the applicants satisfied or met the statutory requirement they would be free to marry. Such an approach might result in hardship for a couple who 'just failed' to satisfy the statutory requirement, but in our view that is to be preferred to the hardship which is likely to flow from uncertainty in the

law. Furthermore, if our recommendations are implemented an application which failed would result in a delay only and would not be a permanent prohibition on the couple marrying.

201. If suitable criteria or guidelines could be devised a subsidiary matter would remain to be resolved, namely whether a judicial process or an administrative procedure would be better able to decide whether the criteria have been met by the applicants. The choice of procedure would largely depend on the particular statutory requirements to be satisfied. Matters of age and time are crucial to the recommendations which we make. For example a requirement that the applicants have attained a minimum age, which is more than the general minimum age (16) at which a person may otherwise lawfully marry, we have referred to as an *age-bar*. Alternatively a requirement that a minimum period of time has elapsed, between the date of cessation of any relationship in which the younger person had been a child of the family of the older person and the date on which notice of intention to marry is given by the couple concerned, we have referred to as a *time-bar*.

202. The choice of mechanism – an administrative procedure or judicial process – is of concern to the Group. We are anxious that any procedure to enable a couple to be exempted from the general law ought to be as simple and inexpensive as possible and an administrative procedure operated by the superintendent registrars and clergymen is most likely to meet these requirements.

203. A requirement involving an age-bar would be a matter capable of being established beyond doubt by production of the applicant's birth certificate. For a not inconsiderable number of people in this country this may be difficult e.g. for those persons, now permanently resident in this country, who are from Commonwealth countries where a comprehensive and satisfactory system for the registration of births has not always been in existence. If an administrative procedure were to be recommended applicants who could not produce the necessary documents to superintendent registrars or clergymen would

have to apply to a court. If the court were satisfied that the applicants had attained the minimum age it could issue the parties with a certificate which would constitute satisfactory documentary evidence to enable the superintendent registrar or clergyman to officiate and arrange for the marriage to be solemnized.

204. A requirement involving a time-bar would have to be the subject of a judicial process. Time, i.e. a period of time since a child of the family relationship ended, is less easily established by documentary evidence and it is a matter which would be in doubt or dispute in some instances. It should be for the Lord Chancellor to decide which court should have jurisdiction in these matters. Our preference would be either the Family Division of the High Court or the County Court. If the Court were satisfied that the statutory requirements had been met, it could issue to the parties a certificate which would constitute satisfactory documentary evidence for the superintendent-registrar or clergyman.

205. One final matter affects possible procedural approaches and that is jurisdiction. Whether it is an administrative procedure or a judicial process that is decided upon it would seem desirable to prevent persons from other countries coming here and marrying in order to circumvent a restriction in their own country. A simple way to achieve this would be to incorporate into any necessary legislation a clause in comparable terms to Section 1(4) of the *Marriage (Enabling) Act 1960* which provides that 'this section does not validate a marriage, if either party to it is at the time of the marriage domiciled in a country outside Great Britain, and under the law of that country there cannot be a valid marriage between the parties'.

# CHAPTER TEN
## Recommendations Touching the Existing Law

206. In making our recommendations we have not found it possible to treat all affines in the same way, and have preferred to consider the relationships in four classes which are as follows:

| Class | Relationships | Figures 1 & 2 (Appendix I) |
|---|---|---|
| A | step-parent and step-child | (3 and 2) |
| B | grandstep-parent and grandstep-child | (5, 6, 9 and 10) |
| C | parent-in-law and child-in-law | (1 and 4) |
| D | grandparent-in-law and grandchild-in-law | (7, 8, 11 and 12) |

207. It will have been apparent that throughout our discussions we have been concerned for the welfare of affines who at some time in the past have been children of the family of an older affine if the child and the older affine should be at liberty to marry.

208. We accept the arguments that where the couple have lived together as members of the same family or household whilst the younger member of the couple was under eighteen years old, the younger person might be at some risk or danger in contracting a marriage which he or she might later regret. We further conclude that although the younger person is not likely to be damaged or hurt in every such instance, the dangers and risks are sufficiently serious for the law, if possible, to afford some protection to the younger person. The heart of the problem, as we see it, is that the younger person would be marrying someone with whom he or she had lived within the same family or household but in an entirely different context – a context of parent and child or grandparent and grandchild. The opportunity for the younger person to decide on marriage

without being unduly influenced by the previous context of the relationship would be prejudiced, unless sufficient interval has elapsed for personal identity and liberty of judgement to be established.

209. A period of delay before the couple could contract a lawful marriage would meet our objective. The delay could be imposed by the law in one of two ways, either by an age-bar or by a time-bar (paras 201 to 204).

210. On consideration of how a delay could be best imposed by law where the younger person has been a child of the family, we have been concerned with two matters. First, the legal and administrative procedures which would be required to establish that the delay required by the age-bar or time-bar had elapsed should be as simple and straightforward as could properly be devised. A time-bar delay may require adjudication of three questions: was the younger person ever a child of the older person's family, when did the relationship of child of the family end, and has the minimum period of time elapsed since the relationship ceased. Certainly in cases of doubt those questions are not capable of being determined by superintendent registrars or clergymen. An age-bar delay would require a procedure to determine whether the parties had both attained the minimum age and, if either of them had not, whether that person had ever been a child of the family of the other person. Thus there would be fewer issues to be determined. In most cases age could be determined administratively. Secondly, we agreed that the consequence of any statutory delay on the lawful marriage of the couple should not be to postpone unreasonably the couple's opportunity to have children in wedlock. Thus we could not accept suggestions for a time-bar of 10 years from the end of the child of the family relationship: in those circumstances the younger person might be 28 years old before he or she could marry. The procedural consequences of an age-bar or a time-bar on the solemnization of marriages are discussed in Chapter 11.

211. What seemed most important to us was for the statutory protection to provide the younger person with time for wider

experience and reflection before he or she married his or her elder affine. Too many young people have discovered to their cost and unhappiness that it is much easier to marry than to divorce. We conclude that, if any restriction should be retained, one based on an age-bar is the least undesirable. A requirement that the younger person had attained a minimum age would avoid both matters mentioned in paragraph 210.

212. There are two other matters which bear upon our recommendations and they both concern age. First a person who has attained the age of 16 years but is below the age of 18 may contract a valid marriage only if the consent of his or her parents or guardians is given (*Marriage Act 1949* section 3). A difficulty may be experienced by a divorced parent where he or she is approached by his or her own child by a previous marriage (and who is still under the age of 18) for consent to marry the parent's second spouse where that second marriage has been terminated by divorce. Similarly, it is difficult to contemplate a step-parent being regarded as capable of giving dispassionate permission for a marriage between himself or herself and a step-child between the ages of 16 and 18.

213. The other matter concerning age is that we do not believe that the law should attempt to protect the older person if he or she is at least 21 years old. There must be some age at which people must normally be regarded as capable of making their own decisions, and we do not see any reason why here, any more than in other circumstances, that freedom should be delayed beyond the age of 21. Historically that has been regarded as the commencement of adulthood even though in recent years the age of majority has for most purposes been reduced to 18. Even this provision is not absolute. It does not apply in the case of a person under 18 years who is a widower or widow (*Marriage Act 1949* section 28(1)). We assume that widowers and widows are exempted from obtaining parental consent simply because they have previously been married.

214. The present law requires that a person under 18 years of age must declare that the necessary parental consent has been obtained.

## Step-relations: Classes A and B

215. The question of a child of the family is of importance when considering whether the existing impediment between step-parent and step-child should be abolished although we recognise that it may also arise when considering the case of grandstep-parent and grandstep-child. It is not exceptional in western society for children to live with and be brought up by their grandparents. This may occur following the divorce, death or illness of their parents. Although no relationship of grandstep-parent and grandstep-child probably existed in the Dare household after 1949,[18] it is worth noting in passing that there were three grandchildren living together in the same household for several years (including several years after Gillian Dare's mother died in 1951).

216.   *We therefore recommend* that:
       the existing legal impediment on marriage between

| Class | a man and his | a woman and her | Appendix I Figures 1 & 2 |
|---|---|---|---|
| A | stepdaughter | stepson | 2 |
|   | stepmother | stepfather | 3 |
| B | father's stepmother | father's stepfather | 5 |
|   | mother's stepmother | mother's stepfather | 6 |
|   | stepson's daughter | stepson's son | 9 |
|   | stepdaughter's daughter | stepdaughter's son | 10 |

should be retained.

217.   Two provisions, however, should be made. The first is to enable a man or a woman to marry his or her affine in the classes A and B i.e. his or her step-parent, grandstep-parent, step-child or grandstep-child, if the younger person has both attained the age of 18 years and has not at any time in the past been a child of the family of the older person.

218.   We have argued that the law ought to seek to protect the younger person where either of the pre-conditions mentioned in the preceding paragraph cannot be met i.e. where the younger person

---

[18]For further information see section in Appendix II entitled *John Francis Dare and Gillian Loder Dare (Marriage Enabling) Act 1982.*

81

(i) is not yet 18 years old;

or (ii) while under 18 has been a child of the family of the older person.

219. If the younger person is not 18 years old (circumstance (i)) the couple should not be permitted to marry. A couple to whom circumstance (ii) applies should be able to contract a lawful marriage, but only after the younger person has attained the age of 21 years. It would be an unreasonable restriction on the couple if the marriage between a man or a woman and his or her affine in the above respective list continued to be prohibited indefinitely.

220. *We therefore recommend* that:

(i) A step-child below the age of 18 should not be permitted to marry his or her step-parent or grandstep-parent.

(ii) Where two persons related by affinity within Classes A and B wish to marry administrative procedures and/or judicial process should be provided:

> (a) to determine whether either person is under 18 years at the date of application;

> (b) to determine whether the younger person has at any time been a child of the family of the older person;

> (c) if the younger person has not at any time been a child of the family of the older person, to issue a certificate permitting the couple to marry in spite of the legal impediment on their marriage;

> (d) if the younger person has been a child of the family of the older person, to issue a certificate to that effect which specifies that the couple may marry on the younger person attaining the age of 21. (The legal impediment would prevent them from marrying until that age had been attained.)

(iii) Where two persons related by affinity within Classes A and B purport to marry other than in accordance with sub-paragraphs (i) and (ii) above, the marriage should be void.

(iv) A person over the age of 21 years should have a complete and unrestricted freedom to marry a person also over the age of 21 years to whom he is related by affinity.

## In-laws: Classes C and D

221. Most, perhaps all, members of the Group started from an intuitive reaction that it was not only unlawful to marry one's mother-in-law or father-in-law, but also that it was undesirable, and perhaps sinful and perilous. But as we studied and discussed the accumulating material we gradually came to recognise that the prohibition is based simply on tradition and cannot now be justified on any logical, rational or practical ground. The experience of other states where there has never been such a prohibition provides a strong and persuasive argument for abolishing these impediments on marriage. In our view, the retention of these legal impediments is not essential to the maintenance of healthy and stable relationships within the extended family. While the possibility of any extreme cases cannot be ruled out they will not undermine the institution of the family in our view.

222. *We therefore recommend* that:
the existing impediment on marriage between:

| Class | a man and his | a woman and her | Appendix I Figures 1 & 2 |
|---|---|---|---|
| C | mother-in-law | father-in-law | 1 |
| | daughter-in-law | son-in-law | 4 |
| D | wife's paternal grandmother | husband's paternal grandfather | 7 |
| | wife's maternal grandmother | husband's maternal grandfather | 8 |
| | granddaughter-in-law | grandson-in-law | 11 & 12 |

should be abolished.

223. The younger person in the above lists will scarcely ever have been a child of the family of the older person before the younger person had attained the age of 18. Moreover, he or she will also have been married (at least once) previously, and for that ceremony the law and society will have treated him or her as having had the capacity and maturity to marry. Thus our

83

principal concern of wishing to afford some protection to the younger person in those circumstances would be satisfied if the existing legal impediments preventing a lawful marriage being solemnized between a man or a woman and his or her affine in classes C and D were removed.

224. Several other reasons were submitted in support of all the existing impediments being retained, but we were not generally impressed by them. None of the relationships in classes C and D involves two persons who are members of the same primary family: their relationships by definition involve at least two such families, even though in some cases one partner of a newly married couple does not leave his or her parental household when establishing the new primary family (Class C). Within Class D, in categories 7 and 8 the two nuclear families will have been connected by the previous first marriage of one or two persons wishing to marry and in categories 11 and 12 the 'connecting' marriage is of the grandchild of one of the two persons. In both Class C and Class D the younger person will already have been married (at least once) before he or she wishes to marry a man or woman within that group.

## The Clergy of the Church of England and the Church in Wales

225. If the main recommendations of the majority of the Group are enacted it will be desirable for the general law to provide a relief to the clergy of the Church of England and the Church in Wales. This desirability arises from the potential conflict between the right of a parishioner to be married in his or her parish church (or the church of a parish on whose electoral roll he or she is enrolled) and the conscience of a clergyman who may regard a particular marriage to be offensive to the teaching or discipline of his church. Other churches and religious bodies have no legal obligation to marry persons who duly present themselves, so it is in regard to these two churches only that the problem arises.

226. It may be that some clergymen will not wish, for conscience's sake, to be legally obliged to marry people who are related by degrees of affinity which are at present an impediment to marriage but which would cease to be so as a result of our recommendations. As explained in paragraph 23, the *Matrimonial Causes Act 1965* gives a relief to the clergy where one of the persons to be married has been divorced (section 8(2)). During the debate on Lady Wootton's *Marriage (Enabling) Bill [H.L.] 1981/82* a proposal for a similar relief was made by way of amendment by the Bishops of Winchester and Norwich, and this was accepted by the Bill's sponsors.

227. *We therefore recommend* that:
if the general law should be changed to permit affines to marry then a relief should be provided to the clergy of the Church of England and the Church in Wales from the obligation to solemnize the marriage of a parishioner with his of her affine.

# CHAPTER ELEVEN
## Possible Consequences for Administrative Procedures

228.   A description of the different procedures for solemnizing matrimony under the present law is given in Appendix III.

229.   Implementation of our recommendation to permit in-laws to marry would not seem to require any changes in administrative procedures, either by superintendent registrars or by clergymen. The change in the substantive law would be made by removing the in-law relations from the First Schedule to the *Marriage Act 1949*. The form of Notice of Marriage (Forms 15 or 17)[19] which superintendent registrars use in ordinary cases would not need to be amended: the declaration which parties at present make would suffice. The declaration is *inter alia* as follows:

> I solemnly declare that I believe there is no impediment of kindred or alliance or other lawful hindrance to the said marriage . . .

230.   Implementation of our recommendation affecting step-relations would require changes. If permission to marry were to depend upon the younger person never having been a child of the family of the older person a declaration that such was not the case would be necessary. The parties might be required to make a declaration in some such form as

> I am related to the other applicant in that she is my wife's daughter by her previous marriage to . . . (*or* he is my husband's son by his previous marriage to . . .) and she (*or* he) has never been a child of my family before she (*or* he) reached the age of 18.

---

[19]The form numbers are those given in *The Registration of Births, Deaths and Marriages Regulation 1968* SI 2049.

(A declaration in reciprocal form might be required of the younger party).

231.   An additional declaration would be necessary if our recommendation were accepted that a party who had been a child of the family of the other party should, in spite of that, be at liberty to marry on reaching the age of 21 – an age-bar. Such a person would be required to make a declaration in some such form as

> 'I am related to the other applicant in that she is my wife's daughter by her previous marriage to . . . (or he is my husband's son by his previous marriage to . . .) but she (or he) has now attained the age of 21, of which evidence is adduced herewith.'

(Here also a declaration in reciprocal form might be required of the younger party.)

232.   A person who makes any declaration which is false renders himself or herself liable to prosecution under the *Perjury Act 1911*. The forms of Notice of Marriage which are used by superintendent registrars carry a warning notice to this effect. This law and this practice should not be changed.

233.   In cases where parties could not establish with certainty whether or not one of them has ever been a child of the family of the other, it would seem necessary for the matter to be determined by a court.

234.   The question though simple to frame could often involve great difficulties in establishing evidence and the absence of adversarial proceedings would seem to indicate the desirability of involving a senior court. Jurisdiction might be given initially to the Family Division of the High Court, with powers for the Lord Chancellor to remit cases to County Courts as a result of accumulated experience.

235.   Proceedings in any court will involve legal costs. We assume that legal aid would be made available for such proceedings but not all couples would be eligible to apply for legal aid (because their income or capital or both exceed the legal aid financial limits). We do not see any way for such a

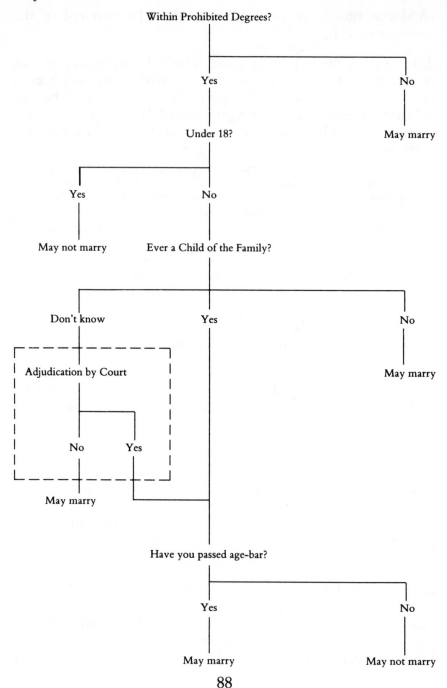

Within Prohibited Degrees?

Yes — Under 18?

No — May marry

Under 18?
Yes — May not marry
No — Ever a Child of the Family?

Ever a Child of the Family?
Don't know — Adjudication by Court
Yes
No — May marry

Adjudication by Court
No — May marry
Yes

Have you passed age-bar?
Yes — May marry
No — May not marry

88

couple to avoid the expense of the legal costs unless they act in person. We hope therefore that the Lord Chancellor, in making any necessary court rules, would encourage the courts to assist couples acting in person who make applications for permission to marry.

236. The decision 'tree' opposite illustrates each step in the procedure consequent upon our recommendations if an age-bar is adopted. Matters to be adjudicated by a court are shown within a dotted 'box'. Other questions could be determined on receipt of satisfactory documentary evidence and the two persons making any requisite declaration before superintendent registrars or the officiating clergyman.[20]

---

[20]See over.

[20]We do not recommend the adoption of a time-bar (para 211). If there were to be provision for a time-bar rather than an age-bar, it would be necessary to establish the fact that a child of the family relationship had once existed and also the date at which it ended, in order that a starting-point could be established from which the qualifying time of the time-bar would commence. Dates may often be in dispute and it would not be within the competence of superintendent registrars, the Registrar-General, or clergymen, to settle these matters. The decision 'tree' would then be as follows:

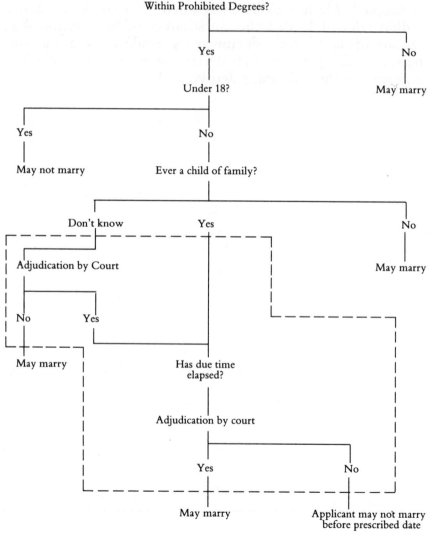

90

# CHAPTER TWELVE
## Principal Conclusions and Summary of Main Recommendations

237. The majority of the Group who sign this Report have reached the following *conclusions*:

1. The procedure by Personal Bill in Parliament is an unsuitable mechanism to decide whether two people should be allowed to marry one another (paragraph 47).

2. To marry is a fundamental human liberty which should be protected. A couple wishing to marry should not be prevented from doing so unless there is some compelling reason or logical impediment. The many particular theological or doctrinal reasons held by particular religious bodies may not for all time constitute appropriate grounds for restrictions against marriage to be embodied in the general law, except insofar as they bear upon the nature of marriage (paragraphs 120-123 and 130).

3. A step-child below the age of 18 should not be permitted to marry a step-parent even if parental permission which satisfies the requirements of the present law is given (paragraphs 212 and 220).

4. There are not sufficient social or psychological reasons to prohibit generally persons related by affinity from marrying if they are aged 18 years and the younger person has never been a child of the family of the older person (paragraphs 217 and 220).

5. There are social and psychological reasons for limiting

permission to marry in circumstances where the younger person has been a child of the family[21] of the older person. We do not consider that this circumstance warrants a prohibition on marriage for all time, but a marriage between such persons should be permitted only after the younger party has reached the age of 21. In all other cases notice of marriage should be accepted once evidence of age has been proved. Thus total abolition of all the existing impediments is not recommended (paragraphs 118, 209, 211 and 218-220).

6. This simple limitation on marriage affects the procedure on giving notice of marriage. It will be necessary for parties to show *either* that they are both aged 21 or over *or*, that if either of them is below that age (but has attained the age of 18) that the younger person has not been treated as a child of the family of the older person (paragraphs 219-220).

7. If evidence of age is all that is required administrative procedures ought to suffice: the process of establishing the liberty to marry must be as simple and inexpensive as possible (paragraphs 210 and 230-231).

8. If the matter of age or the question whether the younger person has ever been a child of the family is in dispute or doubt a judicial process will be required to determine these issues (paragraph 233).

9. Any judicial process should so far as is possible be expeditious and it should not be unduly expensive to the persons concerned or to any intervener. Any decision should be subject to review or appeal. Jurisdiction in these matters should be given to the Family Division of the High Court. The Lord Chancellor should be given discretion to delegate jurisdiction to county courts in the light of experience (paragraphs 204 and 234).

10. Section 8 of the *Matrimonial Causes Act 1965* provides a

---

[21]'Child of the family' is defined on page 3, paragraph 8.

relief for clergymen of the Church in England or of the Church in Wales where one of the parties to a proposed marriage is a divorced person. That present provision would apply to marriages of affines which follow the divorce of one of them. It would seem desirable to extend this relief to all other cases of marriages between affines which might as a result of our recommendations be removed from the prohibitions of the *Marriage Act 1949* section 1 and Part 1 of Schedule 1 (paragraphs 225-227).

11. Any person making a false declaration before a registrar or a clergyman with the intention of evading the limitations of the impediments which remain (for instance by dishonestly representing that although the parties are step-related they had never at any time shared the same household) should be made liable to prosecution under the *Perjury Act 1911*. This is the case at present with other false declarations. The effect upon a marriage contracted as a result of a false declaration about a step-relationship or a child of the family relationship should be to render such a marriage void (paragraph 232).

12. It would be undesirable if the law of affinity differed in any significant degree from one part of the United Kingdom to another. Because the law in Scotland is distinctive, suggestions for changes in the law in other parts of the United Kingdom need to take account of Scots law. It would not be acceptable that conduct which is lawful in England and Wales should constitute a criminal offence in Scotland. This would be the case if our recommendations for the law in England and Wales were followed, and so it would be proper, advisable and necessary for careful attention to be given to the position of Scotland and its law. The *Report of the Scottish Law Commission on The Law of Incest in Scotland (No 69)* Cmnd 8422 is helpful in this direction (paragraphs 30-32).

238. The majority of the Group who sign this Report make the following *recommendations touching the existing law:*

1. the existing legal impediments on marriage between
   step-parent and step-child
   grandstep-parent and grandstep-child
   should be retained subject to administrative and judicial procedures being provided to enable a couple so related by affinity to marry if both persons have attained the age of 18 and at no time has the younger person been a child of the family of the older person (paragraphs 216-219);

2. where two persons related by affinity within the degrees included in 1. above wish to marry administrative procedures and/or judicial process should be provided
   (a) to determine whether either person is under 18 years of age at the date of application;
   (b) to determine whether the younger person has at any time been a child of the family of the older person;
   (c) if the younger person has not at any time been a child of the family of the older person, to issue a certificate permitting the couple to marry in spite of the legal impediment of their marriage;
   (d) if the younger person has been a child of the family of the older person, to issue a certificate to that effect and which specifies that the couple may marry on the younger person attaining the age of 21 (paragraph 220(ii));

3. a step-child below the age of 18 should not be permitted to marry his or her step-parent or grandstep-parent (paragraph 220(i));

4. a person over the age of 21 should be free to marry a person also over the age of 21 years to whom he is related by affinity (paragraph 220(iv));

5. the existing legal impediments on marriage between
   parent-in-law and child-in-law,
   grandparent-in-law and grandchild-in-law
   should be abolished (paragraph 222);

6. if the general law should be changed to permit affines to marry then a relief should be provided to the clergy of the Church of England and the Church in Wales from the

obligation to solemnize the marriage of a parishioner with his or her affine (paragraph 227).

7.  If the general law should be changed to permit affines to marry that permission should not extend to any person domiciled in a country outside Great Britain where, under the law of that country, that person would not be capable of contracting a valid marriage (paragraph 205).

Seear<br>
George Baker<br>
Gordon Dunstan<br>
Ruth Finnegan<br>
Janet Mattinson<br>
Joan Rubinstein

January 1984

# CHAPTER THIRTEEN
## Minority Report

## I. Introduction

239.   We very much regret that we have been unable to sign the majority report. The group as a whole considered that the law is unsatisfactory as it stands at present, especially the personal bill procedure. However, we were unable to agree with the conclusions arrived at by our colleagues in their efforts to find a compromise between the existing situation and the total abolition of the legal impediments to the marriages of affines. We recommend the retention of the existing legal impediments on marriages between step-parent and step-child, step-grandparent and step-grandchild, where the younger person has at any time been a child of the family of the older person. We also recommend the retention of the impediment on marriage between parent-in-law and child-in-law.

240.   The considerations which have influenced us are re-hearsed in the following sections. They arise from differences in interpretation of the evidence submitted to the Group and from the majority's reasoning in three crucial areas, namely the liberty to marry, the value of the family to society and the relationship of the secular to the sacred. Finally we list our own recommendations and conclusions, where they differ from those of the majority.

## II.   Inadequacy of Proposed Provision for Protection of Minors

241.   Throughout our discussions we shared with the rest of the members of the Group a common objective: to discourage

the development of sexual relations between a step-child who is a minor and a step-parent living in the same household. It is our view that the majority recommendations do not achieve this objective.

242.   It was forcefully urged in the House of Lords debates, and again in evidence submitted to the Group from social workers and psychotherapists, that members of any family need the support of clearly defined roles. The case which was most commonly made for retaining the impediment on the marriage of step-parents and step-children was that in this type of family the parent-child role needs to be established and protected. By ruling out the possibility that step-parent and step-child could ever marry, the existing impediment reduces the temptation for them to see each other as likely sexual partners (which implies, of course, the child's seeing his or her natural parent as a sexual rival for the affection of the step-parent).

243.   It has been argued against this point that if a step-parent and a step-child are going to set up a relationship anyway, preventing their future marriage will not deter them. This argument does not convince us. We believe that in most families the well-defined role helps to establish expectations and to create a notion of the appropriate behaviour in advance. Although there may be occasional tragic cases in which erotic interest is aroused in spite of the reinforcement which the law gives to the social role of the step-parent, we think that it is more usual for children to respond positively to affinal prohibitions, and to learn to look outside the family circle for a mate.

244.   The parallel with adoption is a helpful one here. Some step-parents adopt their step-children, one legal effect of which is to make any sexual relations between them incestuous. Presumably they think that this measure, as well as permitting them to share legal rights and obligations with their spouse, will help to secure the new parent-child relationship and establish a basis on which both step-parent and step-child can learn their roles with confidence. If it is appropriate in these

cases actually to enhance the definition of the parent-child relation in this way, we ought to be very careful not to weaken it in the general run of cases. The step-child ought to have securities which are at least comparable with those enjoyed at law by a child who has been adopted.

245. We are of the opinion that the measures proposed by the majority – a delay of up to three years on marriages where the younger person has been a child of the family of the older person – cannot possibly provide the protection which we all wish to ensure for the step-child who is still a minor. The delay between the ages of 18 and 21 is not sufficient to discourage the development of an erotic attachment in childhood. Furthermore, we do not believe that emotional maturity is automatically achieved at 21, and the choice of this as the age at which the child may resolve the confusion of roles between child and spouse does not convince us.

246. As a result of their decision in favour of an age-bar of 21, the majority have, in effect, retreated from the common objective that we shared with them. They speak only of providing 'an opportunity for the younger person to decide on marriage without being unduly influenced by the previous context of relationship' (para 208). But protecting a *young adult* from a precipitate marriage is no substitute for protecting a *child* from a damaging sexual entanglement. We think that it is a proper task of the law to protect children in emotionally threatening situations, and we cannot see why it should hesitate to give protection in this case.

247. Even in protecting the young adult, we consider that the recommendations of the majority are likely to prove ineffective. There can be no 'interval . . . for personal identity and liberty of judgement to be established' (para 208) if for a significant part of the time the couple have lived together in the same home, whether it is still the 'parental' home in a formal sense, or whether the couple have already begun to live as man and wife. Moreover, in those cases where it might need to be established that the child of the family relationship has never existed, we think that the couple will be unlikely to go to the

trouble and expense of making their case at law simply to advance the date of their marriage by a year or two. Couples who were prohibited, or thought they might be prohibited, from marrying at the age of 18 would simply set up home together and proceed to marry when the younger reached the age of 21. Thus we expect that the majority's excellent provisions for the resolution of doubtful cases, if enacted, would remain unused.

248.   If legal obstacles are to exercise a significant influence on people's behaviour, they must be significant obstacles. It is arguable that the general approach which the majority favour could be given more credibility by the substitution of the age of 30 for that of 21. There would be a substantial delay which might act as a dissuasive, but the majority view such a delay as 'unreasonable' (para 210). On the contrary it seems to us that, where the step-child is a minor in the step-parent's family, their relationship as parent and child is of such importance that the timing of a future marriage between them should be governed by the rule which applies in the case of natural parent and child – which is to say, *never*.

## III.   The Liberty to Marry

249.   Although we share the concern of the majority of the group to protect minors, we cannot accept their view that this concern is the only justification for the retention of an impediment. They conceive that there is a prima-facie liberty to marry, with which the law should not interfere except to protect the weak against the risk of serious misjudgement. The affinity impediments, they argue, are an interference with the liberty to marry; they have to be justified therefore in terms of the need for protection, which is to say, as paternalist legislation to discourage the suggestible from making bad mistakes (para 123). This argument has led them to advocate the complete removal of impediments to marriage between in-laws, since the parties must have been adults since their affinal connections began.

250.  The argument does not distinguish clearly between the criminal law and the civil law of marriage. It is a crime to have intercourse with a girl under age, and sexual liberty is restricted in order to protect the vulnerable. It is not a crime for a man to live with his daughter-in-law as man and wife (except in Scotland: see paragraphs 26-32); but to be married in the eyes of the law it is not sufficient for them to live together: they have to secure society's acceptance of their relationship.

251.  The effect of the existing affinal impediments is to express a common refusal to acknowledge such marriages. This is the effect of the law of marriage as a whole: it defines what is, and what is not, marriage, and so legally constitutes the status of marriage in our society. The criminal law also bears on the field of marriage (as, for example, making bigamy a crime), but the law of marriage does not create categories of crime: it establishes categories of social status – married and unmarried.

252.  The law of marriage therefore functions differently from criminal law and does not restrict our liberties in the same way – indeed, our liberties depend on it, for if there were no legal definition of marriage, there could be no liberty to marry which was recognisable at law. We need not be afraid, then, for the law of marriage to make definitions, and to stand firmly by the best account of marriage that can be established.

253.  In para 130, the majority state that the freedom of the individual to marry may be limited or defined by law where the restriction protects not only the individual but also the institution of marriage for the benefit of all persons in the land. We welcome this principle but cannot reconcile it with the more radical proposition of paragraph 129 that freedom to marry should be restricted in as few cases as possible. We are not persuaded by the arguments given there that a couple who at present are prohibited from marrying but decide to live together should be enabled to marry for the sake of the legitimacy of any children they may have. Such a proposition strikes at the roots of our concept of marriage and of the purposes of the law of marriage. If taken to its logical

conclusion it would be a powerful argument for abolishing all affinal impediments to marriage. The Group as a whole stopped short of this conclusion, but the majority have gone further towards it than we could.

254. The majority has been influenced by the anthropological evidence which showed a great variety of affinal restrictions in different cultures and communities. What impresses us, however, is not so much the variety as the consistency with which affinal restrictions of some kind are observed. In our own society the general agreement that an adopted child should be treated under the rules applying to consanguinity suggests that the absolute prohibition on marriage between close consanguineous relations may have more than biological reasons behind it, and may also be designed to safeguard family relationships. We consider that family relationships are under-valued by the majority and our recommendations are an attempt to rectify this, in support of the family itself and in recognition of the importance of the family in society.

## IV.  The Value of the Family to Society

255.  During its discussions the Group has tried to make some assessment of importance of roles within the family. The majority conclude that definition of role in practice counts for less than what individuals – or individual families – make of these roles, and that what is made of them varies too much to provide any norm as a reliable point of reference (paras 97, 99, 108, 109).

256.  In contrast we believe that there is a general consensus in society as to particular definitions, and that implicit definition of role operates both as a safeguard to the stability of the family and as a potential enhancement of it. Further we believe that some specific relationships in the family are free to flourish and convey benefit precisely because they are grounded on the assumption that certain roles preclude sexual expectations. First and foremost among these is the relationship between

parent and child; but the relationships between grandparent and grandchild, brother and sister, aunt or uncle and nephew or niece are also released by the exclusion of sexual overtones to take on their distinctive qualities. These qualities make such relationships intrinsically valuable and also add to the value of family life as a whole.

257. We have already discussed the importance of role-definition between step-parent and step-child. But we believe that this is not the only relationship which would suffer if the recommendations of the majority were implemented: other roles would be weakened, less directly but no less damagingly. To license marriage between a step-parent and a step-child of the family would be to condone sexual rivalry between father and son, or mother and daughter, which, within the close confines of the family, would be destructive of the father and son, or mother and daughter, relationships. In other words, the law would be seen to condone an assault on family relationships which are recognised as essentially valuable ones.

258. The force of this argument drives us to our conclusion about in-laws, for marriage between parent-in-law and child-in-law would have the same effect. In addition, it would deprive the child-in-law of his or her safety of place as child in the new family into which he or she marries. When, for instance, a son brings his wife to his father's home, there is an underlying assumption that the daughter-in-law will assume a role in relation to her father-in-law which is exempt from sexual expectations. To admit the possibility of a future marriage between parent-in-law and child-in-law would be to undermine assumptions which make for the safety and comfort of the adult family.

259. With regard to sexual rivalry between parents and children, it is true that 'the law alone cannot prevent such cases arising' (para 100). But we suggest that this argument invalidates the usefulness of all law. The law alone cannot prevent dangerous driving, for instance: but it can reflect society's wish that lives should be protected and at the same time exert an influence on the consciousness and behaviour of

the vast majority of drivers. It is not, therefore, that the law alone can prevent sexual rivalry arising between parent and child, but that the law as it now stands reinforces a taboo which makes for the safety and well-being of the family in an area of special significance.

260. It will be seen that our disagreement with the majority recommendations rests primarily on two points: first, that the value of relationships within the family is a matter for the law's concern not only when children are children in years but also when they are adults; secondly, that certain relationships, which are valuable in themselves and valuable as contributing to the identity and worth of family life, are in fact too valuable to be sacrificed to a demand which regards the promotion of marriage *per se* as paramountly important.

261. Though our concern here has been mainly with the adult family we must also express our anxiety about the younger children in families that would be affected by the majority recommendations. The issue is raised in paragraphs 56 and 109, but it appears to have been left unresolved.

262. When for instance a husband leaves his wife to live (perhaps in the same neighbourhood) with his wife's daughter by a previous marriage, the children of the present marriage see their step-sister assuming the role of their mother in relation to their father, and their father assuming the role of brother-in-law to themselves. There are many elements here which are likely to cause special distress. The atmosphere of family acrimony may far exceed the acrimony caused when a father lives with another woman who has had no previous place in the primary family; difficulties of access of father to children may be more acute; the disapproval or repugnance of neighbours may be sensed by the children more painfully. Additional role-conflicts and accompanying distress may attach to any child of the union between father and step-daughter. In such a situation we believe that confusion of role and its attendant elements demand something more than 'the kind of coping with personal relationships which people are generally able to resolve in their own lives' (para 109). If the law dignified such

103

liaisons with the status of marriage, the law would seem to countenance unions which by their very nature must disrupt the network of supportive relationships on which family life depends.

263.   The question remains whether society itself endorses our own view of family relationships, which may be thought to be pitched too high; and whether society would wish such a view of the family to continue to be protected by law.

264.   We believe that our view corresponds with a notional view of the family which is widely held and widely valued by society. If the television-viewing public may be taken as representative of society at large, it is significant to note how many popular television series rely on their viewers' recognition of defined roles within the family. Piquancy of effect when characters deviate from the norm would be lost on a public that accepted no premises about how parents and offspring *ought* to behave. In real life individual parents may abuse their parental role by cruelty or indifference to their children, and vice versa; but the idea of what a father or mother stands for, what a son or daughter stands for, is still prized in the general mind, and still retains a tenaciously powerful place in the instincts of society.

265.   Family feeling is impossible to measure. But impressions of a rootless society received from the London press may be misleading and untypical of, for example, the country north of the Trent. In a society which now tends to find itself disconcerted by the fluidity of marital and sexual relationships, the family as an institution acts as a binding factor where marriage as an institution is powerless to bind, and we suggest that the uncertainties now attaching to the marriage relationship reinforce the value which society sets on family or 'fixed' relationships. If marriage is dissoluble, and easily dissoluble, there is still safety in the framework of family relationships which bring comfort by their very indissolubility.

266.   To recommend that certain liberties of choice should be curbed in order to protect the integrity of the family

seems to us to be consonant with the value that society still sets on the family; and to retain the prohibitions we recommend as a minority is not so much to go against the grain of libertarianism as to safeguard an institution which libertarians (as well as countless others) rely on.

## V.  Sacred and Secular

267.  The third area in which we differ from the thought of the majority is the relationship of the secular to the sacred. More precisely, it has to do with the proper place of Christian thought in shaping suggestions for the law of a secular society. The Archbishop of Canterbury, in his terms of reference for the Group, asked it to consider 'theological, sociological and legal issues' in its deliberations. Our concern is that the thinking of the majority has been directed rather to the sociological and legal issues than to theological considerations.

268.  This is certainly not to be attributed to careless indifference on their part, but is, in some measure, a matter of principle. They are anxious to establish a distinction between the sacred and secular realms of practice, between the 'particular marriage disciplines' operated by different religious groups and the 'general or secular law of marriage' (see especially paras 76, 122; but note also para 50, where the distinction has influenced their interpretation of evidence submitted to the Group by religious bodies). Their view appears to be that the scope of confessionally Christian thought is limited to the sacred realm of practice; therefore it had to be largely excluded from the Group's considerations, which were only to do with secular law. Thus they 'do not feel it necessary . . . to come to any view or conclusion upon theological or religious considerations put forward' (para 122); and they mention as examples of such considerations (on which they need not form a view) two Biblical points of reference which figured prominently in Christian discussions of our question in the past: the doctrine that marriage makes a couple 'one flesh', and the prohibition of certain affine marriages in the Old

105

Testament legal corpus. This is followed by a qualification which may soften the initial sharpness of this distinction. But the impression conveyed, both by the paragraphs which make this distinction explicitly and even more by the absence of a theological dimension from the general argument, is that the Christian conception of marriage is a purely sectarian matter which can have no place in a discussion of the law for 'a plural society comprising different religious and cultural groups' (para 76).

269.   This impression is confirmed by the two instances at which the majority refer directly to Scripture in their report. In paragraphs 78-81, where they go into some exegetical detail to argue that Saint Paul's condemnation of the immoral couple at Corinth (1 Corinthians 5:1) is not relevant to the Group's question. The exegetical argument is itself unpersuasive – for the force of the text is not determined by the precise sense of the verb *echein*, but by the description of the offence as an 'immorality such as even pagans do not tolerate' – a description which can only refer to the affinal relationship of the couple. But more revealing than their exegesis of this one text is the general statement against religious influences on secular law by which they introduce it (para 76). From this it appears that 1 Corinthians 5:1 could not be germane to their considerations anyway, whatever the correct exegesis might be. An allusion to Jesus' teaching in the Gospels occurs in paragraph 121 in the course of an argument designed to establish – 'in a long tradition of enlightened rationalism' – the principle of the freedom to marry. They admit in so many words that the Gospel texts are actually silent on this subject, and so contribute nothing to the point which is being made.

270.   Yet, as we have indicated (para 268 above), they allow a qualification to that principle which *might* have turned their minds in another direction. In declining to 'come to any view or conclusion upon theological or religious considerations' (para 122) they add the caveat: 'except insofar as they bear upon the nature of marriage, and why the freedom to marry is to be regarded as a natural right'. The second part of this provision

makes no concession, of course, since it merely allows the religious tradition to be plundered for arguments in support of a modern theory of natural rights. But the former clause might have amounted to an extensive admission of Christian theology. After all, most of what the great Christian thinkers of the past thought and said about marriage falls within this description. They thought a great deal about the nature of marriage – about its ontology and about its importance for human existence – and very little about the form of 'particular marriage disciplines' (para 122). Such Christian thinkers were not legislators of church order, but students of human nature and experience. If their reflections had been part of the Group's discussions, we might have found more common ground.

271. Our own view on the question of the secular and the sacred is simply stated. We accept the distinction between the secular and sacred realms of practice, and do not think that the law of the land ought to be a simple transcript of the law of Christ. Yet we do not think that the two laws can be utterly insulated from each other. Even in modern society, where it is neither possible nor desirable for legislators to presume a general adherence to Christian morality, Christian perspectives on marriage are relevant not only to questions of church order, but also to the shape of secular law. This is because they illumine something of the fundamental structure of marriage in human nature and experience, something which no law, secular or sacred, can afford to overlook.

272. We believe that our view is in keeping with the traditional Anglican conception of the church's role in society (which is not to be confused with the legal and constitutional matter of the establishment of the Church of England). This conception has been characteristically developed in the past with a reference to 'Natural Law'. That term is, of course, capable of misunderstanding in the modern world. 'Natural' is not to be contrasted with 'Christian', as though we were to stop thinking as Christians when we considered secular affairs. What 'Natural Law' meant for Anglican thinkers of the past was an attempt to grasp the structure of natural relationships in

107

a comprehensive way, in the light of Biblical faith and understanding. It assumed that Scripture and Christian tradition were friends, and not rivals, to moral reasoning, and that Christian love needed to be informed by an understanding of how the created order worked. Thus Christian thinkers were free to discuss secular matters in a way that did not forget their secularity but was still authentic to the confession of Christian faith. They did not have to treat the world tyrannously as though it were the Church, but they did attempt, precisely in thinking about the world, to make use of all the understanding which the Christian faith had to offer.

## VI.  Some Legal Considerations

273.   Our recommendations require no different legal procedures from those set out in the majority report. Where step-parents and step-children have never been in a child of the family relationship they may give notice of their intention to marry to a superintendent registrar. Where there is doubt about the child of the family relationship, the majority recommendations provide a procedure for the determination of this question. We agree with their recommendations that all such issues should be entrusted to the Family Division of the High Court, and thus support conclusions 8 and 9. We have already indicated that we recommend that there should be no relief from the existing impediments of marriage between a step-parent and a step-child where there has been a child of the family relationship. Consequently the provisions suggested for the resolution of doubtful cases will be, in our opinion, of greater significance to our recommendations than to those of the majority.

274.   The exemption which we recommend for step-parent and step-child relationships, in cases where there has been no child of the family relationship between two persons, is of no assistance in considering the matter of marriage between in-laws (para 221f). We do not agree with the majority's recommendation to abolish the impediment on all marriages

between in-laws: we believe that the existing impediment must be retained to prohibit the marriage of a parent-in-law and a child-in-law. We would not oppose such marriages in principle if the intervening spouse were dead for then our concern about disruption within the family circle would lose some of its immediate force. However, we accept that it would not be sensible for us to recommend what we would most like to put forward, namely that in-laws should not be permitted to marry until after the death of the intervening spouse. Since the *Marriage (Enabling) Act* 1960 there has been no distinction in the law of affinity between a marriage terminated by death and a marriage dissolved by divorce. We regret the removal of this distinction but we acknowledge that it is unrealistic to contemplate going back to it.

275.   Although we recognise that the arguments against the marriage between parent-in-law and child-in-law can be extended to the marriage of grandparent-in-law and grand-child-in-law we do not think the matter of much importance in the second generation and therefore would not resist the abolition of the impediment in this case.

## VII.   Principal Conclusions

276.   We are happy to associate ourselves with conclusions 1, 2, 3, 8, 9, 10, 11 and 12. We do not subscribe to conclusions 4, 5, 6 and 7 and in their place substitute the following conclusions:

4. The marriage of step-parent and step-child should be permitted if they are both over 18 years of age, provided that proof can be given that they have never effectively lived together such that one was a child of the family of the other. If a child of the family relationship has existed at any time, the existing legal impediment should not be removed with the result that step-parent and step-child should not be able to contract a lawful marriage at any time.

5. Marriages between grandstep-parents and grandstep-children should be treated similarly.

109

6. The existing legal impediments to marriage between parent-in-law and child-in-law should not be removed.

7. The legal impediment on the marriage between grandparent-in-law and grandchild-in-law is of minor significance.

## Recommendations Touching the Existing Law

277.  Referring to the summary of recommendations (para 238), we accept Recommendations 1, 2(a) (b) (c), 3 and 6. We do not subscribe to Recommendations 2(d), 4 and 5 and in their place substitute the following recommendations:

4. The existing legal impediments on marriage between grandparent-in-law and grandchild-in-law should be abolished.

5. Other existing legal impediments on marriage between affines should be retained.

Robert Hart
Ruth Hook
Oliver O'Donovan

January 1984

# APPENDICES

I  Figure 1 – Prohibited degrees of consanguineous and affinal relationships
Figure 2 – Prohibited degrees of affinal relationships: common names.

II  A description of each of the relevant Bills in Parliament since 1979.

III  A description of the procedures for the Solemnization of Matrimony under present law.

IV  Forbidden degrees for marriage in Scotland. *Marriage (Scotland) Act 1977* – section 2 and Schedule I.

V  The Channel Islands and the Isle of Man.

VI  Anthropological evidence: a summary of main points and extracts of evidence submitted.

VII  List of individuals, organisations and institutions which have submitted evidence to the Group.

# APPENDIX I

**Figure 1**

Prohibited Degrees of Consanguineous and Affinal Relationships

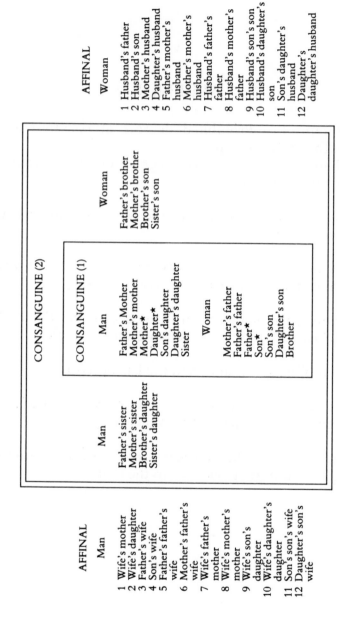

CONSANGUINE (2)

CONSANGUINE (1)

**AFFINAL**

**Woman**

1 Husband's father
2 Husband's son
3 Mother's husband
4 Daughter's husband
5 Father's mother's husband
6 Mother's mother's husband
7 Husband's father's father
8 Husband's mother's father
9 Husband's son's son
10 Husband's daughter's son
11 Son's daughter's husband
12 Daughter's daughter's husband

**Woman**

Father's brother
Mother's brother
Brother's son
Sister's son

**Man**

Father's Mother
Mother's mother
Mother*
Daughter*
Son's daughter
Daughter's daughter
Sister

**Woman**

Mother's father
Father's father
Father*
Son*
Son's son
Daughter's son
Brother

**Man**

Father's sister
Mother's sister
Brother's daughter
Sister's daughter

**AFFINAL**

**Man**

1 Wife's mother
2 Wife's daughter
3 Father's wife
4 Son's wife
5 Father's father's wife
6 Mother's father's wife
7 Wife's father's mother
8 Wife's mother's mother
9 Wife's son's daughter
10 Wife's daughter's daughter
11 Son's son's wife
12 Daughter's son's wife

*Includes adoptive or former adoptive relations

# Figure 2

## Prohibited Degrees of Relationship
Affinal Relatives: Common names

| Man | Woman |
|---|---|
| 1 Mother-in-law | 1 Father-in-law |
| 2 Stepdaughter | 2 Stepson |
| 3 Stepmother | 3 Stepfather |
| 4 Daughter-in-law | 4 Son-in-law |
| 5 Father's stepmother | 5 Father's stepfather |
| 6 Mother's stepmother | 6 Mother's stepfather |
| 7 Wife's paternal grand-mother | 7 Husband's paternal grand-father |
| 8 Wife's maternal grand-mother | 8 Husband's maternal grand-father |
| 9 Stepson's daughter | 9 Stepson's son |
| 10 Stepdaughter's daughter | 10 Stepdaughter's son |
| 11 Granddaughter-in-law | 11 Grandson-in-law |
| 12 Granddaughter-in-law | 12 Grandson-in-law |

The numbers in Figure 2 correspond to those for affinal relatives in Figure 1

Figures 1 and 2 were produced by Robert Chester (Senior Lecturer in Sociology) and Martin Parry (Lecturer in Law, Solicitor) of the University of Hull.

# APPENDIX II

## A Description of each of the Relevant Bills in Parliament Since 1979

1.   In 1979 the Baroness Wootton of Abinger introduced a *Marriage (Enabling) Bill*. Her reason was the increased number of divorce cases and the consequent increase in the numbers of people within affinal relationships who wish to live together with or without the legal and religious sanction of marriage. She instanced a number of actual cases of which she had knowledge. This Bill and others which followed it increased interest in this area of law. A short examination of the purpose of each Bill – both the Private Members' and Personal ones – will be helpful.

### Marriage (Enabling) Bills [H.L.] 1978/79 and 1979/80

2.   These two Bills were introduced in the House of Lords by the Baroness Wootton. The first one completed the Committee stage. It provided for the repeal from Part I of Schedule I of the *Marriage Act 1949* of the twelve relationshps of affinity (paragraphs 15 and 16). A marriage contracted by a person and any of that person's relations by affinity would not by reason only of that relationship be void or voidable had the Bill been successful. The object of the Bill was therefore the complete abolition of the prohibited degrees of affinity. The first Bill was lost on the dissolution of Parliament for the General Election. Lady Wootton introduced an identical Bill later in 1979 but it was defeated on Second Reading on 14 June 1979.

114

## Edward Berry and Doris Eilleen Ward (Marriage Enabling) Act 1980

3.   Mr Berry is the step-father of Mrs Ward. The salient facts were that at the date of her marriage to Mr Berry, the late Mrs Berry was a widow who had previously borne four children by her first and only other husband. Mrs Ward was one of those children. Mr and Mrs Berry were happily married for some 34 years until Mrs Berry died in 1977. Upon his marriage to Mrs Berry in 1943, Mr Berry assumed responsibility for the care and upbringing of his wife's younger surviving children but not of Mrs Ward; Mrs Ward had herself married about one month earlier. Her husband, Mr Ward, died in 1965. After Mrs Berry died in 1977, Mr Berry and Mrs Ward formed the wish to be married to each other. At the time the Bill was introduced Mr Berry was aged 62 years and Mrs Ward was aged 58 years. They lived apart and did not wish to live as man and wife unless they were permitted to be, and were, married to each other.

Second Reading: 22nd May 1980    Royal Assent: 17th July 1980


## Marriage (Enabling) Bill [H.L.] 1980/81

4.   This Bill was in the same form as the two previous *Marriage (Enabling) Bills,* the second of which had fallen by six votes, and it too was introduced in the House of Lords by Lady Wootton. The progress of the Bill was notable for the degree of involvement of the Bishops of the Church of England. The *Second Reading* took place on 25th February 1981.

5.   In *Committee* an amendment by the Bishop of Winchester, supported by the Bishops of Norwich and Carlisle, was lost (by 28 votes to 50). It would have excluded from the provisions of the Bill affines who had been children of the family. An amendment to exclude all persons below the age of 21 years was carried. A further amendment to require the consent of a court after a consideration very close to that provided by the law in New Zealand was easily lost (21 to 40), the Bishops of

115

Norwich and Southwell being in support of it, but the Bishop of Winchester against it. The Bishop of Winchester proposed a clause to relieve clergy of the Church of England or of the Church in Wales from being compelled either to solemnize a marriage between affines or to permit the use of their churches for such marriages, and this too was agreed to.

6. However, opposition was still strongly felt by the Bishops and the motion to receive the Bill on *Report* from the Committee was carried with a thin majority only (36 to 32), with the Bishops of Exeter, Hereford and Norwich opposing it. The Bishop of Norwich introduced an amendment to remove from the provisions of the Bill any proposed marriage either party to which had at any time during the previous 10 years been accepted by the other party as a child of his family, reserving all the time the right to oppose the Bill further. His amendment was again lost (24 to 37), though his two fellow bishops supported him. An amendment giving relief to the clergy, similar to the one moved in Committee, was agreed to; but the three Bishops opposed unsuccessfully the inclusion of a new clause dealing with the application of the Bill to Scotland.

7. So, as Lady Wootton's bill came to its *Third Reading* it was drafted so as to repeal the provisions of the *Marriage Act 1949* which prohibit marriages between in-laws, and to remove the prohibitions on marriage with step-relations if they had reached the age of twenty-one. The clergy were relieved of the obligation to marry such step-relations (but not the in-laws) and to permit the use of their churches for such marriages. The law of Scotland was to be amended in parralled terms. For the bishops Dr Habgood, now Archbishop of York but then Bishop of Durham, expressed opposition. He felt that the Bill would further erode the concept of the family as an extended network of relationships; it would introduce a further element of uncertainty into the already difficult relationship between step-parents and step-children; it would put Britain (he said) out of line with the great majority of European and English-speaking countries; he would not have been unhappy with some way of retaining the legal safeguards in most instances

while providing a way of dealing with what he called 'genuine hard cases'. His views prevailed in the House, and the Bill was defeated in a high vote by 124 to 79. Opposed to it were also the Bishops of Carlisle, Chelmsford, Chichester, Guildford, Lichfield, Peterborough, Southwell, Truro, Winchester and Worcester, and also Lords Coggan, Macleod and Hailsham as well as other prominent lay peers from many churches.

## Marriage (Step-parents and Step-children) Bill [H.L.] 1981/82

8.   This Bill was introduced in the House of Lords by the Lord Lloyd of Kilgerran. Unlike the Bills introduced by Lady Wootton this Bill did not attempt to abolish the prohibited degrees of affinity. Its scope was limited to that of step-parent and step-child and it sought to provide a procedure in the Family Division of the High Court or in any County Court for leave to be given to a step-parent to marry his or her step-child, notwithstanding that they stood in relation to each other within the prohibited degrees of affinity. The Bill did not attempt to abolish any of the prohibited degrees. No leave would be given unless the Court was satisfied that neither party had caused or contributed to the cause of any divorce by the other party and that at no time had the parties 'lived together in a family during the minority of the stepchild'. The test for the court to apply was whether the intended marriage would be 'for the welfare of the parties' and in exercising its discretion the court was to have regard to all the circumstances of the case.

9.   The Bill was approved on Second Reading (22nd February 1982) but did not proceed beyond that stage. After the Bishop of Hereford had announced the Archbishop of Canterbury's intention to set up to a Group to examine the matter (paragraph 5), Lord Lloyd withdrew the Bill.

## Hugh Small and Norma Small (Marriage Enabling) Act 1982

10.   Mr Small is the stepson of Mrs Small. The salient facts

were that Mr Small's father, the late Mr Small (senior), had married in his lifetime three times. Mr Small was the second child of the first marriage which was dissolved by a decree of divorce in 1960. Mrs Small was the late Mr Small senior's third wife whom he married in 1967. There were two children of that marriage who, in 1981, were not yet 18 years old. At the time of that marriage the present Mr Small was aged approximately twenty-four years old and was living separately from his father. The marriage was ended by the death of Mr Small senior in 1981. Throughout most of the period of that marriage, Mr Small worked abroad and had little contact with Mrs Small or her two children. Although Mrs Small is technically Mr Small's stepmother he had never been treated by her as a child of her family. After Mr Small senior died in 1981, Mr Small and Mrs Small formed the wish to be married to each other. Mrs Small's two daughters liked Mr Small and readily accepted their mother's wish to marry him. Mr Small and Mrs Small lived apart and did not wish to live together as man and wife unless and until they were permitted to be, and were, married to each other. At the time the Bill was introduced they were both aged 39 years.

Second Reading: 4th March 1982. Royal Assent: 27th May 1982.

## John Francis Dare and Gillian Loder Dare (Marriage Enabling) Act 1982

11.   Mr Dare is the stepfather of Mrs Dare. The salient facts were that before her marriage to Mr Dare, the late Mrs Dare had previously given birth to a child whilst unmarried. Gillian Iles, later Dare, was that child. At the time of Mr Dare's marriage to the late Mrs Dare, Gillian Iles was in the care of her maternal grandparents who presented Gillian Iles as their own daughter and undertook full parental responsibility for her. Mr Dare and the late Mrs Dare were happily married for some 14 years until the late Mrs Dare died in 1951. There were two children of the marriage. In or about 1949 Mr Dare and the late Mrs Dare together with their two children went to live with

118

the late Mrs Dare's mother with whom Gillian Iles (then aged about 17 years) still lived. The reason for the move was that the late Mrs Dare was ill with cancer and the move enabled her to be cared for in the last days of her illness by her own mother. After her death in 1951 when Gillian was 19 years old, Mr Dare and his two children (then aged 11 years and 6 years respectively) continued, except for an interval of about one year, to live as part of the same household with the late Mrs Dare's mother and Gillian. That arrangement continued until the late Mrs Dare's mother died in 1957 and for some time afterwards. Other members of the Dare family also resided at the same house. After the death of the late Mrs Dare, Gillian Iles cared for the two children and continued to do so until they grew up and left home. During these years Mr Dare and Gillian Iles formed a deep and enduring affection for one another. In 1961 John Dare bought a house and he and Gillian Iles and the two children formed a separate household. Gillian was then 29 years old. In 1971 she adopted the surname Dare and since then has lived openly with him as his wife. At the time the Bill was introduced Mr Dare was aged 66 years and Gillian Dare was aged 49 years. Mr Dare's two children, who were now 41 and 36 years respectively, supported their father's wish to marry their stepsister.

Second Reading: 4th March 1982. Royal Assent: 27th May 1982.

# APPENDIX III

## A Description of the Procedures for the Solemnization of Matrimony Under Present Law

1. The Marriage Acts 1949-83 prescribe the methods by which a marriage may be solemnized in England and Wales. In this Appendix the *Marriage Act 1949* is referred to as the 'Act'. If any persons 'knowingly and wilfully' marry in breach of the procedures and requirements of the Act the marriage is void (sections 25 and 49).

### Marriage According to the Rites of the Church of England

2. Part II of the Act provides that a marriage may be solemnized according to the rites of the Church of England –

(a) after the publication of banns of matrimony;

(b) on the authority of a special licence of marriage granted by the Archbishop of Canterbury (a 'special licence');

(c) on the authority of a licence of marriage granted by an appropriate ecclesiastical authority (a 'common licence');

(d) on the authority of a certificate issued by a superintendent registrar.

A short description of the procedure of each of these methods follows.

AFTER THE PUBLICATION OF BANNS OF MATRIMONY

3.   There are perhaps 12,000 Church of England clergymen who are authorised to conduct marriage, in contrast to the 900 or so superintendent registrars and their deputies who work under the guidance of the office of the Registrar-General. For the purposes of completing an entry in the marriage registers the same particulars are required as in the case of marriages before superintendent registrars. The Church of England does not require a standard form to be used for the collection of particulars. Ecclesiastical printers sell suitable forms but the extent and regularity of their use is not known or controlled (Annexure C p. 128). However, the clergy of the Church of England, no less than superintendent registrars, are expected to take care in establishing the necessary particulars. They commonly regard interviews with the couple as pastoral occasions and probably devote a great deal more time to the interview than superintendent registrars are able to give. If they are alert to possible deceptions by the couple, or mistake, they should be as successful as are superintendent registrars in avoiding them. The Registrar-General issues to incumbents periodically a handbook of *Suggestions for the Guidance of Clergy*. Its present contents are largely legal and administrative requirements concerning registration of marriages.

4.   The procedure for giving notice and publication of banns of matrimony is set out in the Act. The marriage must be solemnized in church within three months after the completion of the publication of the banns, after which period the publication is void (section 12(2)).

BY SPECIAL LICENCE

5.   Enquiries are made on behalf of the Archbishop of Canterbury and the applicants must confirm by affidavit that there is no impediment of relationship, kindred or alliance to hinder the proceeding of the marriage before his special licence is granted. Marriage by special licence may be solemnized in any place and at any time but it must, of course, be according to the rites of the Church of England. Guidance is issued by the Registrar of the Faculty Office to clergymen and applicants.

## BY COMMON LICENCE

6.   Applicants for a common licence make an affidavit before a surrogate of marriages or the registrar of the diocese that there is no impediment of relationship, kindred or alliance to hinder the proceeding of the marriage. Certain clergymen are surrogates. Marriage by common licence must be solemnized in church. The affidavit covers similar matters to those included in the solemn declaration (paragraphs 2-5 of Annexures A or B). Guidance is issued by the registrar of the diocese directing surrogates to explain what is meant, and to remind parties of the penalties of perjury.

## MARRIAGE ON THE AUTHORITY OF A SUPERINTENDENT REGISTRAR'S CERTIFICATE

7.   Part III of the Act provides that the following marriages may be solemnized on the authority of a certificate of a superintendent registrar –

(a) a marriage in a registered building;

(b) a marriage in the superintendent registrar's office;

(c) a marriage according to the usages of the Society of Friends or Quakers;

(d) a marriage according to the usages of the Jews.

## MARRIAGE IN THE OFFICE OF THE SUPERINTENDENT REGISTRAR

8.   The majority of marriages solemnized on the authority of a superintendent registrar's certificate or certificate and licence are conducted in his office and are commonly called civil marriages or register office weddings. The superintendent registrar deals with the administrative preliminaries to the marriage.

9.   The procedure for giving notice is set out in the Act and section 28 provides that no certificate or licence may be issued by a superintendent registrar unless the notice of marriage is accompanied by a solemn declaration in writing made by the person giving notice –

(a) that he or she believes that there is no impediment of kindred or alliance or other lawful hindrance to the marriage;

(b) in the case of a marriage intended to be solemnized without licence, that the persons to be married have had their usual places of residence within the registration district(s) for seven days, or in the case of a marriage intended to be solemnized by licence that one of the persons to be married has had his or her usual place of residence within the registration district for fifteen days;

(c) where one of the persons to be married is not 18 years old and is not a widower or widow, that the consent of the parent or guardian or court has been obtained.

10. Notice of intention to marry is given to a superintendent registrar. Particulars of the couple are carefully compiled by the superintendent registrar. Standard forms[22] are used. They are completed by the superintendent registrar as a result of questions he puts to the couple. Each person is asked to state name, age, occupation, residence, and period of residence. Each person is asked 'Have you ever been through any form of marriage before in this or any other country?'. Enquiry as to place and date of birth may be made of some persons and where either party is below the age of 23 years information as to the date and place of birth is positively required. Evidence is required of the termination of any previous marriage of either person. Where divorce has been in an English court, the decree absolute is required to be produced. A person who is below the age of 18 (but above the minimum age for marriage) is required to provide evidence of the consent of any parent or guardian whose consent is necessary. Again, standard forms are used and the authority for marriage will not be issued until the superintendent registrar is satisfied by written confirmation that the necessary consents have been given. A full birth certificate (in order to prove parents' names) and any court

---

[22]Examples of the forms currently used by superintendent registrars are set out as Annexures A and B to this Appendix (pages 126 and 127). The forms are prescribed by *The Registration of Births, Deaths and Marriages Regulations 1968* (SI 1968 No 2049).

order granting custody which might establish the names of any persons whose consent is required by law is expected to be produced in those cases.

11. In order to assist the parties to make the solemn declaration (see paragraph 2 of Forms 38 and 39: annexures A and B) superintendent registrars may provide informal guidance as to what constitutes legal impediment and have available for reference Tables of prohibited degrees of consanguinity and affinity. The couple are warned that failure to state the particulars truly may render them liable to prosecution. This warning is also displayed prominently in the office of the superintendent registrar.

12. After notice of marriage has been given and the authority or authorities for marriage issued the marriage may be solemnised. The superintendent registrar conducts the ceremony and the Registrar of Births, Deaths and Marriages also attends. Alternatively the marriage may be solemnised by an authorised person in a registered building and once again the couple are required to declare that they know of no lawful impediment to the marriage. The procedures are very full, and very carefully conducted. They are not, of course, proof against deception by either person to be married, or mistake. Cases of each arise from time to time in most offices.

13. The marriage must be solemnized within three months from the date on which notice is given, after which period the authority of a superintendent registrar's certificate or licence is void (section 33(2)).

MARRIAGES NOT SOLEMNIZED IN THE SUPERINTENDENT REGISTRAR'S OFFICE

14. The procedure for giving notice, publication and the issue of a superintendent registrar's certificate for marriage solemnized in a registered building, or according to the usages of the Quakers and Jews, is very similar to that in the case of civil marriages.

15. Marriages may be solemnized on the authority of a superintendent registrar's certificate according to the usages of the Jews or Quakers or in places of religious worship which have been registered for marriages otherwise than according to the rites of the Church of England.

16. Since 1971 the *Marriage (Registrar General's Licence) Act 1970* has enabled a marriage to be solemnized in an unregistered building on the authority of a licence granted by the Registrar General. Provided that he is satisfied that one of the persons to be married is seriously ill and is not expected to recover and cannot be moved to a registered building, the Registrar General's licence is given subject to a similar solemn declaration to the one made under section 28 of the Act except that there is no minimum residential requirement.

17. The *Marriage Act 1983* enables a marriage of a person who is house-bound by reason of illness or disability or is in hospital or prison to be solemnized on the authority of a superintendent registrar's certificate. The certificate is granted under Part III of the Act.

ANNEXURE A

**MARRIAGE ACCORDING TO THE LAW OF THIS COUNTRY IS THE UNION OF ONE MAN WITH ONE WOMAN, VOLUNTARILY ENTERED INTO FOR LIFE, TO THE EXCLUSION OF ALL OTHERS**

# NOTICE OF MARRIAGE BY CERTIFICATE WITHOUT LICENCE.—*(Pursuant to the Marriage Act 1949 and 1954)*

*(Form prescribed by the Registration of Births, Deaths and Marriages Regulations 1968)*

**Form 38.—For Persons each of whom is either 18 years or over, or, if under 18, a widower or a widow**

## PARTICULARS RELATING TO THE PERSONS TO BE MARRIED

| Name and surname (1) | Age (2) | Marital status (3) | Occupation (4) | Place of residence (5) | Period of residence (6) | Church or other building in which the marriage is to be solemnized (7) | District and county of residence (8) |
|---|---|---|---|---|---|---|---|
| | | | | | | | |
| | | | | | | | |

To the Superintendent Registrar of the district of ................................................................ in the county ................................

1. I, the above-named .................................................... give you notice that I and the other person named above intend to be married by certificate without licence within three months from the date of entry of this notice.

2. I solemnly declare that I believe there is no impediment of kindred or alliance or other lawful hindrance to the marriage, and that I and the other person named above have for a period of seven days immediately preceding the giving of this notice had our usual places of residence within the districts named in column 8 above.

3. And I further declare that I am not under the age of eighteen years or, if under that age, am a widower or widow, and that the other person named above is not under the age of eighteen years, or, if under that age, is a widower or widow.

4. I declare that to the best of my knowledge and belief the declarations which I have made above and the particulars relating to the persons to be married are true. I understand that if any of the declarations are false I MAY BE LIABLE TO PROSECUTION UNDER THE PERJURY ACT 1911.

5. I also understand that if, in fact, there is an impediment of kindred or alliance or other lawful hindrance to the intended marriage the marriage may be invalid or void and the contracting of the marriage may render one or both of the parties GUILTY OF A CRIME AND LIABLE TO THE PENALTIES OF BIGAMY OR SUCH OTHER CRIME AS MAY HAVE BEEN COMMITTED.

(Signed) ................................................

In the presence of ................................................  Date ................................
(Signature of registration officer)

Official designation ................................................

Registration district of ................................................

Place of residence ................................................

*NB—Read the other side; in certain cases the additional notice (III) or declaration (IIII) must be completed.*

126

**MARRIAGE ACCORDING TO THE LAW OF THIS COUNTRY IS THE UNION OF ONE MAN WITH ONE WOMAN, VOLUNTARILY ENTERED INTO FOR LIFE, TO THE EXCLUSION OF ALL OTHERS**

# NOTICE OF MARRIAGE BY CERTIFICATE WITHOUT LICENCE. —*(Pursuant to the Marriage Act 1949 and 1954)*

(Form prescribed by the Registration of Births, Deaths and Marriages Regulations 1968)

**Form 39.—For Persons either of whom is under 18 years and not a widower or widow**

## PARTICULARS RELATING TO THE PERSONS TO BE MARRIED

| Name and surname (1) | Age (2) | Marital status (3) | Occupation (4) | Place of residence (5) | Period of residence (6) | Church or other building in which the marriage is to be solemnized (7) | District and county of residence (8) |
|---|---|---|---|---|---|---|---|
| | years | | | | | | |
| | years | | | | | | |

To the Superintendent Registrar of the district of .................................................................. in the county ..............................

1. I, the above-named .............................................................................. give you notice that I and the other person named above intend to be married by certificate without licence within three months from the date of entry of this notice.

2. I solemnly declare that I believe there is no impediment of kindred or alliance or other lawful hindrance to the said marriage, and that I and the other person named above have for the period of seven days immediately preceding the giving of this notice had our usual places of residence within the districts named in column 8 above.

3. And I further declare that in respect of myself ............................................... and in respect of the said‡ ...............................

*(i) the consent of † ........................................ whose consent only is required by law has been obtained;

(ii) the necessity of obtaining the consent † ....................................... has been dispensed with as provided by law;

(iii) there is no person whose consent to my marriage is required by law;

(iv) I am over the age of eighteen years or if under that age am a widow/widower.

*(i) the consent of † ........................................ whose consent only is required by law has been obtained;

(ii) the necessity of obtaining the consent † ....................................... has been dispensed with as provided by law;

(iii) there is no person whose consent to his/her marriage is required by law;

(iv) he/she is over the age of eighteen years or if under that age is a widow/widower.

4. I declare that to the best of my knowledge and belief the declarations which I have made above and the particulars relating to the persons to be married are true. I understand that if any of the declarations are false I MAY BE LIABLE TO PROSECUTION UNDER THE PERJURY ACT 1911.

5. I also understand that if, in fact, there is an impediment of kindred or alliance or other lawful hindrance to the intended marriage the marriage may be invalid or void and the contracting of the marriage may render one or both of the parties GUILTY OF A CRIME AND LIABLE TO THE PENALTIES OF BIGAMY OR SUCH OTHER CRIME AS MAY HAVE BEEN COMMITTED.

Court has consented to the marriage in the space provided

(Signed) ......................................................... Date ....................................

In the presence of ...................................................... (Signature of registration officer)

Official designation ......................................................

Registration district of ......................................................

Place of residence ......................................................

* Delete the alternatives which do not apply (eg. if none applies) insert the appropriate declaration as to consent in the space provided

† Insert the name(s) of the person(s) whose consent is/are required

‡ Insert the name of the other party

*NB—Read the other side; in certain cases the additional notice (II) or declaration (III) must be completed.*

# Banns of Marriage Application

PLEASE READ

This form may be completed by one of the partners on behalf of both.

Only the sections marked * need be completed if the marriage is to take place in another parish.

The notes overleaf are important and should be read before each section is completed.

| | 2 *Full name (block capitals) | 3 *Age at proposed date of wedding | 4 *Condition (strike out what does not apply) | 5 Rank, profession, or occupation | 6 *Address at time of publishing banns (and telephone no.) | 7 Father's full name (if deceased add deceased) | 8 Father's rank, profession, or occupation |
|---|---|---|---|---|---|---|---|
| (Man) | | | Bachelor / Widower | | | | |
| (Woman) | | | Spinster / Widow | | | | |

| | 9 Nationality | 10 Date of birth | 11 Have you been previously married? | 12 If so, was the previous marriage terminated by death? | 13 Have you been baptized? If so, where? | 14 *Since when have you lived at the address in 6 above? | 15 *Which is your parish church? |
|---|---|---|---|---|---|---|---|
| (Man) | | | | | | | |
| (Woman) | | | | | | | |

| | 16 Are you related, or connected by marriage? If so, how? | 17 *At what church do you wish to be married? | 18 *On what date? | 19 At what time? |
|---|---|---|---|---|
| (Both) | | | | |

*I hereby certify that to the best of my belief the answers to the above questions are correct.

Signature

Signature

Date

Future address

For use by clergy

Dates for publication of banns

# APPENDIX IV

## Forbidden Degrees for Marriage in Scotland

### Marriage (Scotland) Act 1977 (c.15), section 2 and Schedule 1

2.(1) A marriage between a man and any woman related to him in a degree specified in column 1 of Schedule 1 to this Act, or between a woman and any man related to her in a degree specified in column 2 of that Schedule shall be void if solemnized –

(a) in Scotland; or

(b) at a time when either party is domiciled in Scotland.

(2) For the purpose of this section a degree of relationship exists –

(a) in the case of a degree specified in paragraph 1 of Schedule 1 to this Act, whether it is of the full blood or the half blood; and

(b) in the case of a degree specified in paragraph 1 or 2 of the said Schedule, even where traced through or to any person of illegitimate birth.

(3) Where a person is related to another person in a degree not specified in Schedule 1 to this Act that degree of relationship shall not, in Scots law, bar a valid marriage between them; but this subsection is without prejudice to –

(a) the effect which a degree of relationship not so specified may have under the provisions of a system of law other than Scots law in a case where such provisions apply as the law of the place of celebration of a marriage or as the law of a person's domicile; or

(b) any rule of law that a marriage may not be contracted between persons either of whom is married to a third person.

## SCHEDULE 1

## Degrees of Relationship

*Column 1*                                    *Column 2*

### 1.   Relationships by consanguinity

| | |
|---|---|
| Mother | Father |
| Daughter | Son |
| Father's mother | Father's father |
| Mother's mother | Mother's father |
| Son's daughter | Son's son |
| Daughter's daughter | Daughter's son |
| Sister | Brother |
| Father's sister | Father's brother |
| Mother's sister | Mother's brother |
| Brother's daughter | Brother's son |
| Sister's daughter | Sister's son |
| Father's father's mother | Father's father's father |
| Father's mother's mother | Father's mother's father |
| Mother's father's mother | Mother's father's father |
| Mother's mother's mother | Mother's mother's father |
| Son's son's daughter | Son's son's son |
| Son's daughter's daughter | Son's daughter's son |
| Daughter's son's daughter | Daughter's son's son |
| Daughter's daughter's daughter | Daughter's daughter's son |

## 2.   Relationships by affinity

Mother of former wife

Daughter of former wife

Former wife of father

Former wife of son

Former wife of father's father

Former wife of mother's father

Mother of father of former wife

Mother of mother of former wife

Daughter of son of former wife

Daughter of daughter of former wife

Former wife of son's son

Former wife of daughter's son

Father of former husband

Son of former husband

Former husband of mother

Former husband of daughter

Former husband of father's mother

Former husband of mother's mother

Father of father of former husband

Father of mother of former husband

Son of son of former husband

Son of daughter of former husband

Former husband of son's daughter

Former husband of daughter's daughter

## 3.   Relationships by adoption

Adoptive mother or former adoptive mother

Adopted daughter or former adopted daughter

Adoptive father or former adoptive father

Adopted son or former adopted son

# APPENDIX V

## The Channel Islands and the Isle of Man

1. The *Marriage Act 1949* does not extend to the Channel Islands or the Isle of Man. Acts of Parliament do not apply to either the Channel Islands or the Isle of Man except by express mention or necessary implication. (None of these islands forms part of the United Kingdom.) Thus the law of marriage in those islands is a matter for local legislation.

2. There are special arrangements covering the forms and ceremonies required for marriages. When a marriage is intended to be solemnised or contracted either in England or Wales or in the Channel Islands or the Isle of Man between a British subject resident in any of those islands and a British subject resident in England or Wales, a certificate for marriage issued in England or Wales by a superintendent registrar or a certificate of publication of banns or a certificate of notice of marriage issued in accordance with the local laws is sufficient (*British Subjects (Facilities) Act 1915*, section 1(1)).

# APPENDIX VI

## Anthropological Evidence: A summary of Main Points and Extracts of Evidence Submitted

1. Among other material, the Group took note of statements submitted by anthropologists. This appendix gives extracts from those statements together with some passages from the earlier paper by Professor B. Malinowski to which reference is made. This is preceded by a summary of the main points which were found of particular relevance in the group's discussions.

### Summary of main points

2. All societies have certain rules and prohibitions concerning both marriage and sexual relations, though their specific nature varies from culture to culture.

3. Prohibitions on marriage and/or sexual relations between close blood relations are universal or near universal, though the precise definition of this close family and the interpretation of such prohibitions vary according to the culture and may not correspond precisely with our own ideas. The reasons for this widespread prohibition are still a matter of controversy among anthropologists, but some suggested explanations (among others) are the potentially disruptive effects of erotic interest within a close family living together (a reason stressed in Malinowski's statement, below) and the need to protect young children from sexual exploitation by those in authority over them.

4. Prohibitions on marriage or sexual relations between affines (those related through marriage rather than blood) are more varied and often less stringent than those within the immediate family. Such prohibitions must be seen in the context of the historical circumstances and the wider social relations of the society concerned. They tend to be more important in societies in which people live together in larger joint kin groups, and in which permanent affinal relations are set up on marriage between the two families or kin groups as a whole, than they are in the kind of situation more typical of contemporary Britain where couples normally try to set up their own separate households on marriage, where marriage does not normally set up a permanent relationship between whole families, and where affinal ties between individuals may not outlast the marriage which brought them into being.

5. There are also many minority cultural groups in Britain whose differing systems of marriage rules should also be considered (as in E. Goody's statement below). Some are more, some less, concerned with rules governing relations between particular affines.

6. It would be difficult to use the anthropological evidence to forecast precisely the likely results of any change in the law. This is partly because there is still academic debate about the analysis of marital and sexual rules and the significance of prohibitions in various situations. Nor is it easy to predict with certainty whether or how far any changes in the law would directly affect general attitudes to affinal relations. It does seem reasonably clear however from E. Goody's paper (as well as from the statements we received concerning various minority religious groups such as the Sikhs) that whatever the law, certain groups of individuals may well choose to retain their own system of rules and prohibitions where these are more stringent than the law of the land in theory would permit.

## 7. Extracts from statements by anthropologists

A. Concluding sections of 'A sociological analysis of the

rationale of the prohibited degrees in marriage' by Professor B.
Malinowski, as submitted to the *Commission on Kindred and
Affinity as Impediments to Marriage* (published 1940;
Malinowski's paper appeared as Appendix 3, pp 101-106).
B.   *The marriage of step-relations* by Professor J. S. La Fontaine
(London School of Economics), on behalf of the Royal
Anthropological Institute.
C.   *Current patterns of affinity with special reference to marriage of
step-relations among immigrant groups in Britain*, by Dr E. Goody,
(New Hall, Cambridge), on behalf of the Association of Social
Anthropologists of the Commonwealth. (Extracts only; the
full paper includes a discussion and description of patterns
among West African and ex East-African Gujarati immigrants
in Britain.)
D.   *The legalisation of marriage between step-relations* by Dr Sybil
Wolfram (Lady Margaret Hall, Oxford). (Dr Wolfram's main
evidence is printed, omitting certain illustrative tables and
additional papers.)

**A.   A Sociological analysis of the rationale of the
prohibited degrees in marriage** Professor B. Malinowski
(excerpt). Reproduced from *Report of the Commission on Kindred
and Affinity as Impediments to Marriage* (1940 SPCK)

(8).   '. . . Marriage prohibitions are not absolute, with the
exception of the prohibition of incest, which is universal.
Prohibited degrees depend on the nature of social organisation.
Wherever we have a group of people who normally live
together, or at least co-operate and develop a type of solidarity
on the family basis, marriage is prohibited for the members of
such a group. For, let us remember, the prohibition of
marriage means a bar to erotic interests, to sexual preliminaries, and it also brands illicit sexual relations as morally
heinous. The permission of marriage, on the other hand,
invites, as it were, erotic approaches and attitudes of courtship.
Wherever, owing to close joint life, temptations of sexual
attractions naturally occur, a clear 'Yea' or 'Nay' is necessary
on the part of law, morals and religion.

(9). A few words only are necessary to cover the nearest extension of family ties. The aunts and uncles (mother's sister and father's sister; father's brother and mother's brother) naturally act in many cases as substitute parents. In primitive communities the extensions of family appellations very often document and express this important fact. In such communities we have the clear distinction between maternal and paternal lines, so that only the brothers and sisters of the relevant parent assume the character of substitute parents and are prohibited in marriage. In such societies, unlike our own, first cousins on the relevant side are also strictly forbidden to marry, since they are regarded as brothers and sisters.

(10). Let us pass now to the most problematic aspect of prohibited degrees: the bar on marriage between people related to each other through their own spouse. Let me take concretely Nos. 17 and 18 on the list of prohibited degrees – that is, the wife's sister or husband's brother, the brother's wife and sister's husband.

(11). If the above theory is correct, there exist good reasons for such prohibitions. This is based on the principle that the permissibility of a future marriage implies at least the possibility of courtship during a present marriage. Under social conditions, where a wife's sister shares her home with a married couple, the husband would assume the position of authority and protectiveness towards her, and naturally there creep in certain intimacies of daily life, just because the woman stands to the man in the relation of an adoptive sister. Is any possibility of erotic or sexual attitude to be allowed to creep in or not? On the line of absolute safety the question would be decided in the negative. The same refers to the prohibitions of marriage between a woman and her deceased husband's brother and similar relations by marriage. A clear case can be made for such prohibitions, but it is also evident that they largely depend on certain sociological conditions and that they embody counsels of perfection.

(12). What are the social conditions under which the stringency of such prohibitions would seem directly indicated?

(13). A few generations ago contacts between men and women were very much more clearly defined on lines of affinity and relationship. Men and women did not mix freely in public life or in private work, in office or business, in co-operation and competition, to the extent to which they do now. Nowadays friendships between people of opposite sex are much more freely struck. The line of demarcation between personal and free intercourse between relatives on the one hand and the very formal and distant type of contact between unrelated people has been largely obliterated. Thus a few generations ago the opportunities of intimacy and erotic temptations which ran on lines of affinal contact were of much greater importance than they are now. We have also to remember that at present the scope of joint-family life has been much more restricted. People are living in smaller households, confined to single families. Thus, considering such prohibited degrees as 17 and 18, but also 6, 7, 8 and 29 and 30 [see note at end of this excerpt], the stringency is lessened: first, because the joint-family life is of far lesser occurrence in present households; secondly, because such inducements to intimate friendship and easy relations are not so much confined now to affinal relations as they were before.

(14). The above argument, contains a number of general principles and implies the solution of a number of problems.

1. The main sociological reason for marriage taboos and prohibited degrees is the elimination of sex from relations of the family type. A group leading a joint life with the intimacy of daily concerns, with the need of an organised authority and unselfish devotion, cannot tolerate within its framework the possibilities of sexual approaches, for these act as a competitive and disruptive force incompatible with the even tenor and stability of the family.

2. From this point of view, legislation and moral influence might regard as the optimum the widest range of prohibitions, including kindred by blood and near affinal relatives. But the legislator and the moralist must remember that the rule not naturally obeyed is bad law. He will therefore have to restrict the prohibited degrees to a well-considered minimum.

3.   None of the rules as laid down by the Church of England would appear to an intelligent sociologist in any way injurious or unjustified. A good case can be made, as a counsel of perfection, even for those which have been most discussed. On the other hand, the prohibition of affinal degrees – notably, 17 and 18, 29 and 30 – may be considered as less stringent under the present conditions. Any divergences between the law of the State and that of the Church are obviously injurious to both.

4.   From the above argument it is clear that the number and nature of prohibited degrees depends on the character of the family, or the joint-family, and on the importance of extended kinship in any given type of society. It also depends on the general nature of relations between men and women; on the degree in which their associations and possibilities of easy friendship are strictly determined by bonds of kinship and affinity, or else, can be formed irrespective of such bonds.

Circa 1939.

(15).   (Note. Key to degrees of affinity referred to by number:

| | |
|---|---|
| 6. father's brother's wife | father's sister's husband |
| 7. mother's brother's wife | mother's sister's husband |
| 8. wife's father's sister | husband's father's brother |
| 9. wife's mother's sister | husband's mother's brother |
| 17. wife's sister | husband's brother |
| 18. brother's wife | sister's husband |
| 29. wife's brother's daughter | husband's brother's son |
| 30. wife's sister's daughter | husband's sister's son) |

## B.   The marriage of step-relations
### Professor J. S. La Fontaine

(16).   The report of a committee established to advise the then Archbishop of Canterbury on *Kindred and Affinity as Impediments to Marriage*, published in 1940, contained an essay by Malinowski, the famous anthropologist. It can serve as a basis for the present discussion but not without some modification.

Today most anthropologists would agree that one must consider the ban on sexual relations between kin of certain categories separately from marriage prohibitions. In any society there are persons between whom marriage is forbidden but sexual relations are not thought to be incestuous. In England for example the criminal offence of incest does not include relations between a man and his step-daughter, nor a man and his adopted daughter, although they may not marry. (The Scottish law does not include the relationship of a man to his illegitimate daughter as one which bans sexual relations between them.) While it is common to find that both incest taboos and marriage prohibitions are justified by reference to the same idea, that of 'close' relatedness, anthropologists do not explain marriage rules by reference to rules regulating sexual relations. In considering the problem of marriage between step-relations, anthropologists would consider it in the context of the system of social relations based on kinship and marriage.

(17). The existence of bans and taboos does not of itself prevent actions which break these social rules. There are a number of cases of incest each year and also a number of cases of offences committed by men against their under-age step-daughters. There does not seem to me to be the evidence which would indicate clearly whether a relaxation of the ban would encourage or discourage such related, illegal behaviour.

(18). Malinowski pointed out that 'the nature and number of prohibited degrees depends on the character of the family or the joint-family and on the importance of extended kinship in any given type of society'. While anthropologists today would probably modify the terms in which Malinowski wrote, they would also agree that evidence from other societies cannot serve as a model for our own society. However, comparison shows widely variant forms of kinship and marriage systems. An example which is relevant comes from Africa: the Zulu of South Africa and the Gisu of Uganda with similar forms of patrilineal kinship have opposed views on the marriage of a man with his wife's sister. Zulu traditionally considered that the love of sisters would prevent the usual rivalry between co-wives; the Gisu considered that the rivalry of co-wives would spoil the love of sisters; the Zulu encouraged sororal polygyny while the Gisu forbade it. The English kinship system terms traditionally assimilated in-laws (affines) to kinsmen and made distinctions between 'near' and 'distant' relations, not differentiating between connections through father or mother, birth or marriage, but only between degrees of relatedness. Marriage and the courtship which preceded it was seen as disruptive of the permanent co-operation, sentiments of affection and rights and duties which constituted such close ties. However the system has not remained unchanged and gradually a distinction between 'blood' ties and affinal ties has emerged and the ban on many affinal relations has been dropped. Malinowski singled out certain categories as 'less stringent under the present conditions': wife's sister, brother's wife, wife's brother's daughter and wife's sister's daughter. The last two resemble the marriage of step-relations in that there is a difference in generations as well as an affinal link.

(19).   While the terminology 'step' singles out certain relations from among affinal relations, this has not always been so. A step-mother was formerly known as a mother-in-law. It is probably the emphasis on the nuclear family of parents and children living independently which has led to the singling out of parents' spouses and those spouses' children in this way. A son's wife is logically as closely related as a father's wife to any man, a daughter's husband as mother's husband, yet son-in-law and daughter-in-law are not step-relations. They fall outside the scope of this enquiry for reasons of social definition not logic.

(20).   A basic characteristic of marriage in almost all societies is that it establishes new relationships, not only between husband and wife but between their kin. Where children are born these relationships endure as kinship ones and do not change if the marriage is broken by death or divorce. These broader affinal ties were formerly a bar to marriage but have been changed so that the implication must be that a married couple are only weakly linked to each other's kin. The most striking demonstration of this is that step-brother and sister may marry. However it should be noted that a change in the rules of marriage will affect not merely certain individuals who may be concerned but their kin: children, siblings and parents.

(21). Marriage establishes rights and claims to services and property in all societies. Where a widow is married by her late husband's kinsman it is often to ensure her support and that of her children or to retain her property and labour for her husband's kin (see E. Goody's paper). Such support may be forthcoming for a widow who is banned from remarriage but no such perpetual obligations are shouldered by affines in modern English society. However such dimensions should be considered: in the case of the marriage of a man and his father's widow, where there are children of the first marriage, who has prior claims to her property?

(22). The modern English kinship system seems to be developing into one in which only primary kin are significant and affinal ties do not outlast the marriages which brought them into being. Logically therefore one should consider the secular view in which marriage may be dissolved by divorce. If a man might marry his father's ex-wife or his ex-wife's daughter would that be acceptable to public opinion? Neither marriage would be incompatible with the tendency of older men to marry much younger women as second wives but might be considered destructive of the relations of father and son, mother and daughter, that is of the remaining kinship ties which retain their social significance.

(23). There exists a body of opinion that the law should be changed but the number of couples affected is likely to remain very small. It is also open to the Government to change the procedure for considering exceptional cases, making it less cumbersome and expensive.

October 1983.

## C. Current Patterns of Affinity with special reference to marriage of step-relations among immigrant groups in Britain
Dr Esther Goody (extract)

(24). It is most appropriate that the Group should seek information on patterns of affinity among immigrants in Britain, as their successful integration depends not only on how they are viewed by the 'natives' but also on their perception of English law as relevant to their values. It is possible, though difficult, to treat English society as having a single system of marriage, and thus as being subject to a single set of marriage laws. However, no such entity as 'the immigrant family' or 'immigrant marriage patterns' exists or can be meaningfully constructed.

(25). This is not simply the splitting of theoretical hairs by an academic. Among the many immigrant groups with substantial numbers settled in this country are those of Hindu, Muslim, Rastafarian and Buddhist faiths as well as devout Christians; those from the Indian sub-continent, from Africa, from the Mediterranean and the Caribbean – each area with its own culture and distinctive forms of social structure – and of marriage patterns. The question then becomes how it is possible to take account of the particular diversity of many different sub-cultures. In this there is no short cut; no alternative to looking in some detail at the main immigrant groups. Given more time it would be possible to seek this information from anthropologists who have worked directly with each of these populations. All that I can do here is provide an account for the two groups with whom I have myself worked in this country. However, even in the absence of comparable material on other immigrant groups these accounts may indicate the *kind* of variation from the English patterns, and between immigrant groups, which occurs. For there are two quite different and highly significant sorts of variation that must be taken into account in any discussion of patterns of affinity in the immigrant populations in Britain:

142

1. There is the variation between immigrant groups – and this often extends to significant differentiation within a group which is perceived by 'us' as unitary.
2. There are the changes which are occurring within each immigrant group as they adapt to economic, religious and social conditions of life in England, and as their children attend English schools and come home speaking a second language, with English friends and English ideas.

These two sorts of variation – internal differentiation and changing norms – are not cited as a caution against generalizing the accounts which follow. They are a critical part of these accounts. It is in the nature of immigrant marriage patterns that they are highly varied, and that they are changing.

(26). [Dr Goody then devotes several pages to describing these patterns among West Africans in Africa and Britain, East-African Gujarati Indian immigrants to Britain, and the Barber Caste in Gujarat, North-Western India and then states a conclusion.]

(27). I have tried to indicate where the problem of marriage to step-parents would fit into the system of regulation of marriage of two immigrant groups in the United Kingdom, West Africans and Gujaratis from East Africa. For neither group is marriage to step-parents currently occurring. In neither group is it central to the pattern of marriage preferences and prohibitions. For each of these groups there are marriages that are very strongly prohibited indeed, but there are others which people are pragmatic about. Marriages to foster- and step-parents probably fall into this latter category, particularly for West Africans. The kinship forms of both West Africans and Gujaratis in this country are undergoing rapid change, though this takes radically different forms in the two populations. For the West Africans the changes are in the directions of closer nuclear family relationships (a more 'closed' family), but this is combined with a relatively high rate of divorce and re-marriage. Classificatory parenthood is less important here in England (though still significant), but step- and foster-parents are a significant occurrence. For the Wallen sub-caste of Gujaratis, changes are in the direction of a more open family pattern, with less dependence between adult parents and children. Conjugal separations are beginning to occur in the parental generations, where this was impossible before. Legal divorce and remarriages must soon follow. More open families, and shifting family relationships will mean more complicated family relationships including step-relationships. It is hard to see this extending to the marriage of step-relatives for a long time to come.

October 1982.

## The Legislation of Marriage Between Step-Relations
Dr Sybil Wolfram (extract)

BRIEF HISTORY OF ENGLISH PROHIBITED DEGREES

(28). Until 1907/8 prohibition of marriage and sexual intercourse in England followed a simple pattern: all relations in or within certain degrees of consanguinity and affinity (both created by sexual intercourse as well as marriage) were forbidden to marry and sexual relations between them was incest. There was a drastic curtailment of their extent during the Reformation to relatives in or within the 3rd degree by the civil law reckoning of degrees, i.e., up to but not including first cousins. At the same time, dispensations, permitting marriage within the prohibited degrees, were discontinued. The practice grew up that marriages within the prohibited degrees were (only) voidable, and could be questioned only by interested parties, and during the lifetime of both partners. Incest, i.e., sexual relations within the same degrees, was dealt with by the ecclesiastical courts and was punishable by public penance/excommunication. In 1835, by Lord Lyndhurst's Act,[23] future marriages within the prohibited degrees became void *ab initio*. Subsequent court rulings also prevented 'marriages' celebrated

---

[23]*Marriage Act 1835*

abroad from rating as valid. The tightening up of the law almost certainly precipitated the 1842-1907 controversy to legalise marriage with a deceased wife's sister. The principal opposition was based on the forecast that since prohibitions on affines (who are blood relations of a spouse or conversely the spouse of a blood relation) rested on the doctrine of the unity of husband and wife (who *inter alia* took on each other's relatives at marriage; and 'being related' implied, *inter alia,* not being able to marry), there would be nothing to prevent the removal of prohibitions between all affines. The 1857 *Matrimonial Causes Act* appears to have terminated the Church of England's jurisdiction over incest.

(29). The legislation of marriage with a deceased wife's sister in England was finally effected in 1907, after being effected in colonial countries. Adultery with a living wife's sister continued to rate as incestuous (and thus as grounds on which a woman could divorce her husband). In 1908 the *Punishment of Incest Bill,* previously rejected, became law and made incest a crime between a narrow set of blood relatives, *viz*: parents and children, siblings, and grandfather and granddaughter. In 1921 the 'anomaly' of forbidding a man to marry his other sister-in-law, his brother's widow, was removed. In 1931 marriage was permitted with all other relatives of a deceased spouse except those in the 'direct line'. The Church of England came into line with Statute law in 1940. In 1960 marriage with the same blood relatives of a divorced spouse was legalised.

(30). The category of 'step-relations' has never specifically featured. There has been no prohibition on marriage or sexual relations between step-brothers and step-sisters. Unlike step-parents and step-children, they are not affines. In England no relationship existed or exists between the kin of one spouse and that of the other, but only between the married couple and the kin on each side. Step-parents and step-children are no more nor less affines than parents and children-in-law. (The 'step' terminology is not new, but 'in-laws' used to be an alternative for parents and children.)

## SOME INFERENCES
*The law*
(31).   The course of events hitherto makes it probable that if there is permission for step-children and step-parents to marry after the death of their spouse, this will be followed by permission both for them to marry after divorce, and for parents and children-in-law to do so. There are also strong signs that sexual intercourse between blood relations will cease to be a crime, whether piecemeal or otherwise (cf e.g., *Working Party Report about Sexual Offences* 1980 HMSO, paras 108-129); and there would then appear no reason to preserve prohibitions of marriage between aunts and nephews, uncles and nieces or closer blood relatives.

(32).   Loopholes such as that of the pre-1835 voidable marriages or dispensations as used by the Roman Catholic Church can stabilise a position for some time, in the past sometimes for centuries. Voidable marriages within the prohibited degrees lasted until 1835. Divorce by private Act of Parliament remained in force *c.*1700-1857. So far as I know, demands for judicial divorce did not become strong until the 1850s, and especially following the (rather biased and inaccurate) Royal Commission of 1853. This was in spite of the fact that England was probably the only Christian country with effectively neither annulment nor divorce as means of terminating a marriage, and that Scotland had divorce from 1560 onwards. However, at present it appears more likely that such methods of dispensation would swiftly be followed by 'legislation'.

*Incidence*
(33).   Like Professor La Fontaine, I think incidence is impossible to forecast. There has been no ban on the marriage of first cousins in England since 1540, but it is still regarded as slightly dubious, suggesting that legalisation need not be accompanied by approbation and that the incidence of legalised marriage/ sexual relations between relatives could remain low. The evidence of the history of divorce in England, however, possibly tells the other way. The rate was rising, albeit slowly,

before its 'legalisation' (making it a judicial process) in 1857. It then jumped from *c*.3.3 p.a. to 150 p.a., and has risen and grown easier to obtain ever since despite the increase being constantly deplored. (It was also being deplored in 1809.) The strong stigma which continued to attach to individual cases has by now disappeared, and it is possible that if no, or almost no, prohibited degrees remained, marriage/sexual relations between relatives would similarly lose their oddity in individual cases, and a similar uncontrollable/deplored general rise in incidence occur. It is worth adding that there seems to have been less concern about incest, etc., at some periods in England in the past than for example around 1908 when incest was made a crime cf. e.g. Defoe's *Moll Flanders* 1722 where full brother-sister marriage is taken lightly. There has, however, always been some prohibition.

(34). Like Professor La Fontaine I am inclined to attribute the already marked change in attitude to unions between relatives to a changed attitude to relationship, whereby it is narrowed, less important, etc. The diminished significance accorded to marriage, of which 'divorce by consent' in the 1970s is a symptom, and to sexual relationship may also have a role, so that their occurrence between relatives appears at present less significant than at some periods in the past.

THE PROCESS OF CHANGING THE LAW

(35). The arguments employed in Commissions, Parliament, etc. in favour of making alterations in laws about matrimonial and sexual matters are commonly that the present system is expensive and open only to the rich, that English law is out of line with that of other countries, especially Scotland (with its very different law in these areas), and that social circumstances have changed. I do not know the present expense of obtaining a private act to marry an affinal relative. In the 1853 *Royal Commission on Divorce*, which was arguing for making divorce a judicial process in England and inexpensive, like Scotland, the then expense was much exaggerated, as was its inaccessibility to the lower classes. 'Legislation' of divorce in England

147

followed, rather than preceded, divorces being obtained lower in the social scale.

(36). Changed composition of the family has often been used as an argument for reducing the extent of English marriage prohibitions, as in your own 1940 Commission. But the evidence suggests that, for at least many centuries, the English family or household has consisted of parents and unmarried children only, as it does now. It has been considered that a married couple should set up its own household, not necessarily in proximity to either parental home. I do not know if there has been a change in distance, and I doubt if there is any substantial evidence on the point, which would in any case need to be offset by changed transport altering the effects of distance.


A BRIEF CONCLUSION

(37). Almost all theories about marriage prohibitions and/or incest turn on some aspect of the household or relatives in proximity, and hence arguments turn on these also. The theories which have been put forward are almost certainly (all) false as explanations or justifications for forbidding (or allowing) unions between relatives, and would be unlikely to prove serviceable in maintaining restrictions as attitudes change. Nor is it clear what causes changed attitudes, such as the far more tolerant one towards unions between close relatives than prevailed only 20 years ago. The theories which have been proffered are not however necessarily exhaustive, and it cannot be inferred from their probable falsity that no ill-effects would result from legalisation of marriage whether between step-parents and step-children or the other relative between whom legalised marriage would be likely to follow.

November 1982.

# APPENDIX VII

## Lists of Organisations and Persons who Submitted Comments in Writing to the Group

Professor Sir Norman Anderson
The Most Rev. J. W. Armstrong, the Archbishop of Armagh
Canon G. B. Bentley
Mr and Mrs E. Berry
Dr Parminder Bhachu
Dr Klaus Bockmuehl (Regent College, Vancouver, Canada)
The late Rt Rev. D. Brown, formerly Bishop of Guildford
Professor W. E. Butler (University College, London)
Juan Luis Cervera (Spain)
R. Chester and M. Parry (University of Hull)
Mr and Mrs J. F. Dare
Pamela Duveen
The Rt Rev. and Rt Hon G. A. Ellison CVO, formerly Bishop of London
Mrs Justice Evatt (Chief Judge, Family Court of Australia)
Professor J. S. la Fontaine (London School of Economics)
Dr Esther Goody (Department of Social Anthropology, University of Cambridge)
The Most Rev. J. S. Habgood, the Archbishop of York (formerly Bishop of Durham)
The Lord Chancellor (Lord Hailsham of St Marylebone)
Mr L. (Hertfordshire)
Lord Lloyd of Kilgerran
Professor Peter Low (University of Virginia, USA)
Douglas McHendrie (Counselor at Law, Denver, Colorado, USA)

Mr John Lucas (Merton College, Oxford)
The Most Rev. H. R. McAdoo, the Archbishop of Dublin
Professor Gilbert Meilaender (Oberlin College, Ohio, USA)
Mrs N. (Kent)
Mr Robin Piper
Marjorie Proops
Professor Paul Ramsey (Princeton University, New Jersey, USA)
Claire Rayner
The Most Rev. K. Rayner, the Archbishop of Adelaide
Rees & Freres (Parliamentary Agents)
Lord Robertson of Oakridge
Mrs Margaret Robinson, (University of London, Chelsea College)
Lady Saltoun
Lord Simon of Glaisdale
Mr H. Small
The Rt Rev. M. Stockwood, formerly Bishop of Southwark
Judge P. J. Trapski (Principal Family Court Judge, New Zealand)
Professor Philip Turner (General Theological Seminary, New York, USA)
Tuomo Weckroth (Lutheran Church of Finland)
Dr Sybil Wolfram (Lady Margaret Hall, Oxford)
Baroness Wootton of Abinger

Association of Chief Probation Officers – Family Law Sub-Committee
Beth Din, London
British Association for the Study and Prevention of Child Abuse and Neglect
British Medical Association
The Buddhist Society, London
The Canon Law Society of Great Britain and Ireland (Monsignor E Dunderdale) and the Catholic Marriage Advisory Council
Christ Church parish, Virginia Water, Surrey
The Church of Scotland (General Assembly)

Family Division of the High Court (Sir John Arnold, President)
The Family Law Bar Association
Free Church Federal Council
The Archbishop Methodios of Thyateira and Great Britain
Home Office
Institute of Family Therapy
The Islamic Cultural Centre, London
The Islamic Foundation, Leicester
The Law Commission
Law Society's Standing Committee on Family Law
London Sevashram Sangha
The Mothers' Union
The National Marriage Guidance Council (Professor Edward Griev)
Nationwide Festival of Light
Scottish Law Commission
Study Commission on the Family (now known as the Family Policy Studies Centre)
The Tavistock Clinic (Mr Neville Symington)